Make-Up Artist's Handbook
for Stage, Screen & Video

MAKE-UP ARTIST'S HANDBOOK
for Stage, Screen & Video

— ■ —

Diego Dalla Palma

 Sterling Publishing Co., Inc.   New York

Cover: Photograph of Gigi Fantoni; make-up by Romualdo Priore.

All drawings are by Salvatore Cibelli except drawings of hairstyles, which are by Diego Dalla Palma.

Translated by Christiana Guarneri.

Library of Congress Cataloging in Publication Data

Dalla Palma, Diego.
　Make-up artist's handbook for stage, screen & video.

　Translation of: Il make-up professionale, teatrale e cine-televisive.
　Includes index.
　1. Make-up, Theatrical. I. Title.
PN2068.D3513　1985　　　792'.027　　　85-12618
ISBN 0-8069-7050-2
ISBN 0-8069-6242-9 (pbk.)

Copyright © 1985 by Sterling Publishing Co., Inc.
Two Park Avenue, New York, N.Y. 10016
Originally published in Italy under the title, "il make-up, professionale, teatrale e cinetelevisivo," © 1982 Ugo Mursia Editore, Milan
Distributed in Australia by Capricorn Book Co. Pty. Ltd.
Unit 5C1 Lincoln St., Lane Cove, N.S.W. 2066
Distributed in the United Kingdom by Blandford Press
Link House, West Street, Poole, Dorset BH15 1LL, England
Distributed in Canada by Oak Tree Press Ltd.
 c/o Canadian Manda Group, P.O. Box 920, Station U
Toronto, Ontario, Canada M8Z 5P9

Contents

Acknowledgments

I wrote this book because someone pushed me into doing it. She was Emma Calderini, the costume designer, one of the finest and kindest people in the profession.

Unfortunately, she won't be able to read it; she is no longer alive. To her, my fondest recollection and all my thanks.

I am most grateful for the help and support of Maud Strudthoff and Marta Roncarati, during the years I spent working for RAI Radiotelevisione in Milan, Italy. I owe them almost everything, both from a professional point of view and often from the human one.

Thanks to Gianna Sgarbossa, my friend, who stood by me through the most difficult times of my career.

I would particularly like to express my appreciation to Dario Piana, one of the most skillful and imaginative artists in television and movie special-effects make-up; to Giancarlo Carniani, a lighting technician much in demand for his knowledge and skill. And again, many thanks to everyone who helped me during these thirty-two years of life.

To you, who are just about to read this book—thank you, too!

This book is dedicated to my father, to my mother, to T.P., and to my colleague Romualdo Priore.

Introduction

In Italian, the word for "make-up" is *trucco,* and it probably derives from an ancient provincial word that means to "cheat" or "trick." *Trucco* is also an ancient game of skill similar to today's billiards. Words don't come about by chance—there's always a reason and a significance for them. Because show-business people and models do a little bit of playing and perhaps a little bit of cheating, they all need to be made up for their work. Make-up is very important to all of them and is often the key to their credibility and success. And, of course, the make-up job depends largely on the ability and skill of the make-up artist to mystify, to trick, and to create.

Make-up not only corrects your features and changes your appearance, but it also enhances your face and makes you look "right." The camera—whether it's shooting in black and white or in color, for television or film—magnifies every blemish, red spot, and birthmark. When you don't wear make-up at all on camera, it's very noticeable. Your face may seem to have an uneven texture, scars, large areas of discoloration, or distracting freckles. It's always advisable to use at least a light make-up to give your complexion an even tone.

For television work, make-up is used minimally, since the screen is so small. Heavy make-up is also not usually used in films these days, because it now looks unnatural to us. On stage, of course, actors need to wear heavier make-up, because they're a greater distance from their audience.

When you're planning to wear any kind of make-up, consult with the person who is coordinating the lighting. It's vital to know what kind of lighting will be used so that you can apply your make-up properly. In my many years of work in the entertainment industry, I've seen some beautiful faces on which make-up—because of inadequate lighting—didn't do much, and some mediocre faces that became wonderful with the help of good lighting. The wrong lighting can illuminate blemishes that the right lighting will conceal.

If you're working in television, and more than one camera is shooting a scene that is lit only from above, doing a good job with make-up becomes difficult. But generally, when you're shooting a movie, the task is fairly simple because the lighting is done only for one take. And it's easier still in the theatre, where you have complete control over the effects as the make-up relates to the colors, the gels, and the filters of the lighting system.

Another factor to take into consideration is the clothing to be worn. Always consult with the designer of a production and make sure that you're trying for the same effect. In Italian television, where the designer develops all the hairstyles and wigs, you can see that this would be crucial. It isn't the same in film work, where sketches and styles of wigs, moustaches, beards and hairpieces fall into the realm of the make-up artist or the hairdresser. Never use a light make-up with dark- or deep-colored clothing unless the script specifically calls for it. Always use make-up sparingly on characters dressed in white or in pastel colors. Avoid sparkling and bright make-ups, unless the script requires them, because they can cause serious problems for the cameramen. Also avoid very intense black-and-white tones, especially for television.

During a telecast, a make-up job is often damaged or changed (sometimes for the better!) after you finish it. It's important to take a quick close look at all the made-up, costumed actors just before a taping or performance, to avoid unpleasant surprises. Keep in mind that the make-up you create should be in delicate shades, because the picture could be transmitted either in color or in black and white. For black-and-white work, you need to use highlights and shadows to make features more defined, but you don't want to overdo it. Always strive to use make-up in moderation.

Besides lighting and costumes, at least part of the success of make-up depends on the cinematography—the settings and the texture of the scene. When all these elements are in harmony with the make-up you design, you'll obtain the most beautiful or appropriate images.

Basic Make-Up Knowledge

It is important for every make-up artist to know anatomy—not only facial anatomy (see Figs. 1–3), but the anatomy of the entire human body. This knowledge helps us to understand how to define each part of the face and form. In fact, as a top-flight make-up artist, you have to be able to construct everything from artificial bones and huge pot bellies to false ears! You need to know how to simulate flabby muscles, prominent veins, and craggy bone structures.

Fig. 1

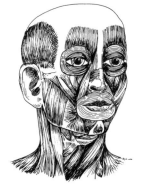

Fig. 2

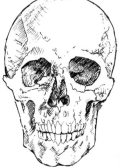

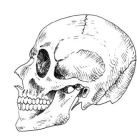

Fig. 3

You will find it helpful to study drawing, sculpture, and painting, to read books about the history of art and see how the masters have done the job over the centuries. The best make-up artists you'll meet in the theatre—or in television and films—always know, even if not proficiently, how to paint and sculpt. This expertise will keep you from falling into the trap of merely powdering already pretty faces rather than exploring the true art that make-up is. In fact, doing make-up can be one of the most fascinating and satisfying of the arts, provided that you approach it and carry it out in a knowledgeable and creative way.

Basically, there are three different types of faces (Fig. 4):

Caucasoid
Negroid
Mongoloid

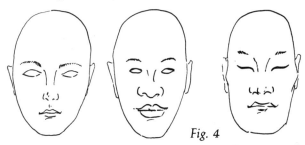

Fig. 4

In order to design any make-up, you need to measure the face in the following way (Fig. 5):

Height: from hairline to eyebrows, to end of nose

Width: the space between the eyes

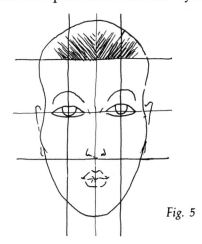

Fig. 5

Experienced make-up artists do this automatically. Instinctively, they know when to "reduce" or "enlarge" a face (Fig. 6), but it's important to consider this consciously when you're just beginning in the craft.

Fig. 6

Another way to study the face is to compare it to the geometric shapes shown in Figs. 7–11. Most faces correspond to one or the other of these shapes.

As a make-up artist, you also need to know about the types of products available. One kind of make-up is for daily use and not recommended for film or stagework. Make-up that is specifically prepared for the stage is far too heavy for street wear. Included in this type of make-up is a range of colors and items as varied as one can imagine, for every possible theatrical purpose.

Generally, the cosmetics used for everyday wear are available locally in a wide variety of shops, while professional make-up is distributed in a limited way and only in large cities. It is necessary to plan your orders well ahead of time and deal with manufacturers who can fill your needs consistently and promptly.

Every make-up artist should own two make-up kits: one containing products for street wear and the other products suitable for film and theatre work. There will be little crossover between them.

In either case, however, it's a good idea to stick with a manufacturer whose products are of high quality with a good assortment of items and a wide color range. Among the best are: Max Factor, Ben Nye, Kriolan-Brandel, Bob Kelly, Makeupstudio, M. Stein, and Mehron.

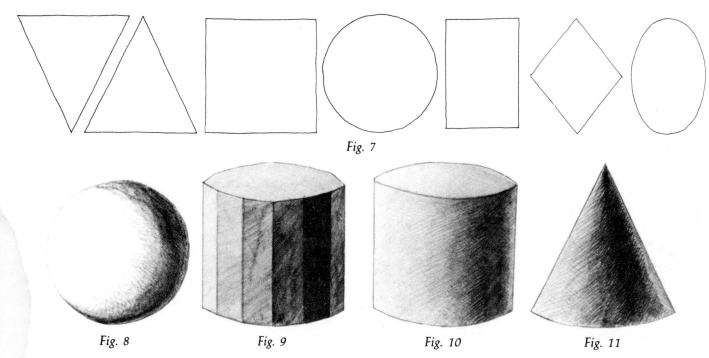

Fig. 7

Fig. 8   *Fig. 9*   *Fig. 10*   *Fig. 11*

Make-up Materials

The following is a list of the items you need to have on hand in your make-up kit:

Acetone Used as a solvent, mostly to clean the nylon edges of nets upon which wigs, moustaches, and other hairpieces are constructed.

Aging glue A white glue that dries transparent and flat, used for creating wrinkles on the face.

Adhesives A wide range are available: dull and bright, creamy and liquid, in tubes and in bottles (spirit gum), on strips and double-stick tape.

Alcohol, isopropyl Used as a solvent and also for creating an artificial tan.

Antiperspirant A liquid you can use on chin, nose, and forehead to avoid excessive perspiration.

Atomizer Used to spray cold water onto the face to set the make-up, and also for other purposes.

Beards and moustaches It's always a good idea to keep a couple of ready-made beards and moustaches on gauze, if you need one in a hurry.

Blades Used for sharpening pencils.

Blood, artificial A red liquid with the consistency of real blood. Artificial blood will do perfectly well for simulating old wounds, and it is also available in waterproof form for scenes that have to be played in or under water. For creating believable wounds, insert artificial blood capsules into a mould or other putty form and place in the mouth and on some other part of the body.

Blot-out A make-up stick used to cover blemishes, shadows, and other imperfections.

Brilliantine Used to flatten and brighten hair.

Brushes In various sizes and bristle softnesses, for eyes, for shadows, for the application of rouge or latex, to remove powder, and for other uses. It's possible to have brushes made of mink, camelhair, and synthetic fibres.

Caps Always have at your disposal latex and plastic caps in different sizes and fairly thin edges. You'll need to use these when you have to give the illusion of age or baldness.

Cleansing pads Small, round pads, dampened in oil, used to remove make-up from the eyes and other sensitive areas.

Combs Used in various sizes, shapes, and materials for brushing eyebrows, separating eyelashes, and other combing needs.

Cotton Useful for creating the effect of very old skin, as well as for the application of putty and other uses.

Creams Creams for dry skin and a lotion for oily skin.

Cream stick A smooth, easily applied foundation make-up in convenient stick form, applied with a dry polyurethane sponge. Available in many shades for stage, film, and video.

Crepe hair and wool Braided hair used to make beards, moustaches, and sideburns. It also can be used to simulate hair anywhere else on the body, applied with spirit gum.

Curler, eyelash Used for curling eyelashes.

Curling irons In various sizes, you can heat them electrically if you're working indoors, and with a special heating tool if you're out on location.

Enamels Nail polish is available in a wide range of colors. Tooth enamels, however, come in only a few shades which have to be mixed together.

Eyelashes, false. Available in different styles: singly, in tufts, and on tape (a very thin thread of transparent plastic).

Eyeliner Available in various dark shades in liquid form, it is used to draw the outline of the eyelid. The cake form has the same properties as liquid eyeliner, but it remains on the skin longer. You need to dilute the color with water to apply it.

Eye shadow Available in every possible shade, the most practical eye shadow is that which comes in compact powder.

Fixative Used to set putty or latex moulds and create a smooth plastic surface on which to apply make-up base. It is available in several forms: The spray leaves a thinner film, and is also used to set imaginative, complex make-ups.

Gel Used to flatten and brighten hair, and for other purposes.

Glitters Synthetic sparkling particles used in special-effect make-ups. Absolutely avoid using glass particles.

Glycerine Used to create artificial perspiration and tears; also for the look of a metallic body.

Greasepaint The basic foundation make-up.

Hair coloring Colored sprays or liquids that provide temporary color changes.

Hairpins, haircombs Available in different sizes for hairstyling.

Hair spray Used to set hair, moustaches, and beards.

Heating tool A device used to heat curling irons. Available in different sizes, they are helpful to arrange a curl, beard, wig, or particular hairstyle.

Jelly A lubricant used when working with putty and flattening hair, and other purposes.

Latex A rubber substance used to create the effects of age, slashes and scars, skin diseases, and also for artificial additions to body and face.

Lifts Little moulds of net or synthetic materials that lift facial muscles, and are also used to attach hairpieces and floppy ears. Skinlike in appearance, they are available on rolls of tape.

Lip gloss A shiny substance that makes lips and other facial areas look extremely bright.

Lipsticks In many colors, preferably in stick form, to be applied by brush. It's best not to choose one that changes the lip color too drastically.

Make-up Used to change body color, it is available in many shades in liquid and cake forms.

Make-up remover A liquid used to remove make-up. A very greasy cream is good for removing stubborn make-up from the face.

Mascara Available in various types of containers and in many colors. It is best to use a waterproof product.

Moustache wax Used to keep moustaches and pointed beards in shape.

Nails, artificial Made of plastic, they attach to the real nails by means of a very strong adhesive.

Netting Used for shaping muscles, lifting them, and for other purposes. It works better for television than for films. You can also use it to construct and ventilate wigs, moustaches, and beards, leaving a small border along the edges. It is a better base for the hairpiece than the silk gauze which is often used.

Oils Used to create the effect of glossy skin. Castor oil is good for softening plaster moulds when you want to draw on them with pencil, or when they start to go limp because of perspiration. Almond oil is excellent for removing make-up quickly.

Pancake A greaseless, water-soluble foundation make-up that you apply with a dampened sponge. Don't use it on dry skin. It's frequently used as a make-up base for men.

Pencils, cosmetic Available in a wide variety of colors, cosmetic pencils can be used to draw on any area of the body, but most of the time they are used on eyes and lips. Choose cosmetic pencils with soft lead, which provide a clean, lasting outline but are easy to wipe off.

Petroleum jelly Used to create an appearance of glossy skin and other effects.

Plastic, liquid This product creates very thin moulds that you can use to cover eyebrows and other parts. It also can be used to construct quick, strong elastic caps for simulating baldness.

Powders Translucent powder is used to complete every make-up and give a matte finish to shiny parts of the face.

Some tints provide creative ways to darken the skin. Rice powder provides a light, sheer finish. Pearly powder gives a deep sheen. Intense colors are available for fashion make-ups and special effects.

Putty A plastic adhesive wax that you can model directly onto a person for temporary changes. It is particularly useful for some facial features, particularly in bony areas, for noses, to simulate floppy ears, and for other purposes.

Rouge Available in various shades in cream and cake forms, it is used for touching up the completed make-up and for adding color to some parts of the face.

Scarring material Used to simulate scratches and scars or give a scaled effect to the skin.

Scissors In various sizes and shapes, to use for trimming eyelashes, crepe hair, netting, etc.

Spirit gum A thin adhesive paste used for attaching crepe wool and hair.

Sponges Synthetic and natural sponges, with flat or rough surfaces, are useful for applying cream, stick, pancake, latex, and for many other purposes.

String Have different colors of string at your disposal for constructing synthetic lifts. Also have some cotton thread on hand to use with gauze lifts.

Tanning lotion Used for creating an artificial suntan.

Tissues For cleaning, drying, obtaining an aged effect, and consolidating latex layers.

Tools, modelling and surgical There are many kinds: orange wood sticks (used by sculptors), metallic tools (used by dentists and doctors), and they are used for many purposes in the make-up room.

Tooth wax Used to create the effect of missing and decayed teeth. It is also used to cover the gums.

Tweezers Available in various shapes and sizes, you'll need them for many purposes, from the application of artificial pieces to face and body and for attaching false eyelashes.

Of course, make-up artists use many utensils and products that they don't carry along with them all the time. Some of these products are needed only for special cases. But all the items listed above should be readily available either in your kit or close at hand. If you are going on location, carefully select everything you might need beforehand, but leave behind useless, bulky items.

The following are helpful notes about some specific items:

Make-up kit Put particular care into keeping your make-up kit clean. Cleanliness and order, besides being your best calling card, will help you to avoid unpleasant, chaotic moments. (More about cleaning things on page 122.)

Cosmetic pencils Shape the lead so it is flat on one side and pointed on the other (Fig. 12). Be sure to protect the point with a cap.

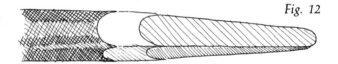

Fig. 12

Brushes The best ones to buy—the ones you'll need most—are the flat ones made of marten, which are used for blending and for applying powders and paste to face and neck. Select a wide variety of sizes, from small thin ones to large fat ones. Also get brushes with different kinds of bristles (mink, ox, sable, camel, Chinese bristles). Synthetic, sponge-tipped applicators are also useful in applying powders and blending eye shadows.

When you buy a brush, make sure that all the hairs are held firmly in the base; you don't want them coming out while you're working. Brushes for face make-up range from #0 to #12 (the most frequently used—Fig. 13); those which serve more limited uses range from #16 to #28. Higher numbers are unnecessary.

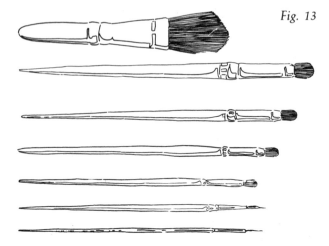

Fig. 13

It's convenient to keep a few small toothbrushes around. Use them for cleaning wig edges, hairpieces constructed on netting, and for many other purposes. You can also use little brushes for eyebrows and eyelashes. A wide assortment is shown in Fig. 14.

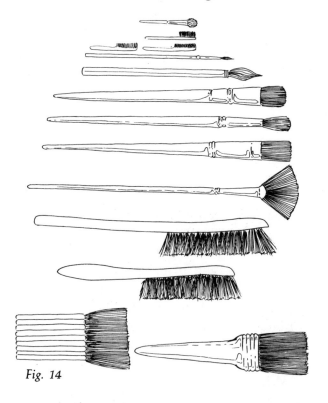

Fig. 14

When you're finished using your brushes with cream stick, pancake make-up, or putty, clean them with shampoo. After using them with latex, wash them with a solution of cold water with two spoonfuls of an ammonia-based liquid cleanser.

Sponges Available in different sizes (foam rubber, red rubber, natural, and synthetic), sponges are indispensable (Fig. 15).

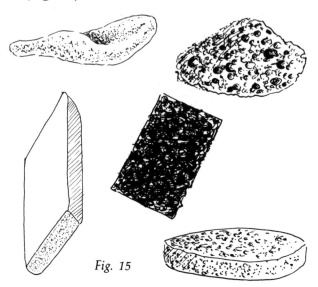

Fig. 15

Always keep a few small- and medium-sized porous sponges for creating the look of natural skin texture on clay or putty. Working with scissors, trim them carefully into a round shape. Then, after you apply the foundation, pat it with the small dry sponges to get an even, natural effect. If you use too large a sponge for this purpose, it will leave an unattractive halo of foundation on your face and at the hairline.

A small natural sponge, dampened in very cold water, serves to set the make-up. Pat the face with it lightly after you apply powder.

Wash foam rubber sponges as infrequently as possible, because they crumble easily. Generally, you'll need to throw them away after five or six washes.

Tools Such tools as tweezers, scissors, and dental instruments (Fig. 16–21) should be cleaned with acetone. Wood spatulas should be washed in hot water and soap. Use alcohol to remove grease.

Setting Up a Make-up Room

Your make-up room should be wide enough for you to move around easily (Fig.

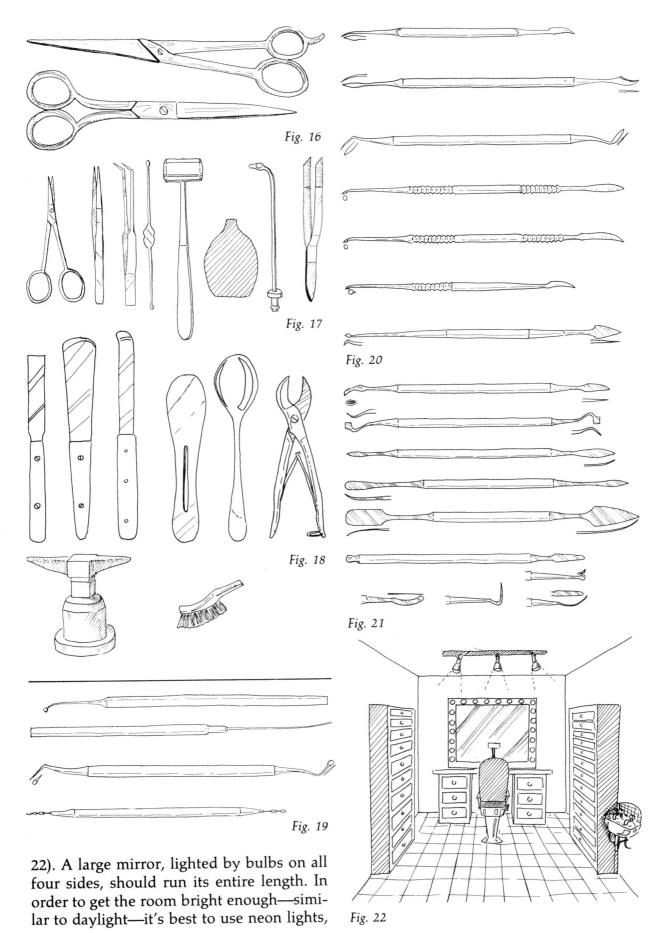

Fig. 16

Fig. 17

Fig. 18

Fig. 19

Fig. 20

Fig. 21

22). A large mirror, lighted by bulbs on all four sides, should run its entire length. In order to get the room bright enough—similar to daylight—it's best to use neon lights,

Fig. 22

which are least likely to alter colors. Three spots should be placed in the ceiling, two steps behind the make-up chair, with the beams directed towards the mirror. It's important for the walls to be painted a neutral color—off-white is good—and that curtains, furniture, and floor are covered with plastic material for practicality and cleanliness.

It helps to have roomy cabinets (again, in a light color) in which to store your equipment.

A comfortable barber's chair makes a great make-up chair.

It is also a good idea to install air conditioning so that you can maintain a normal temperature in hot weather; otherwise, it will be difficult to keep make-up from smudging.

You'll need a sink with running water for dampening and washing brushes, and for other purposes, too.

It is very useful to keep a camera handy so that you can photograph a complicated character make-up and be able to recreate it when you want.

Maintain a notebook in which you keep some forms (you can have them printed in-

---

Production:

Name:

Address:

Telephone:

Telephone number of Production Company, School, or Organization:

Procedures in Order

Highlighting:

Foundation: { **cream stick:**
pancake:
other base: }

Shadowing:

Powder:

Eyes: { **eyeliner:**
eye shadow for the eyebrow bone:
eye shadow for the lid:
eyebrow pencil:
mascara: }

Eyebrows:

Mascara:

False eyelashes:

Lip pencil:

Powder blush:

Lipstick:

Wig:

Special products or notes:

expensively), which list different products and procedures for a particular character's make-up, including the person's name, address, telephone number, and the production involved. It is also useful to keep sketches of make-up jobs you have done

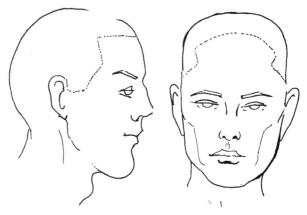

Fig. 23

for future reference. Include a work sheet such as the one on page 18, so that you can list the important data. If you add female and male face shapes, both in profile and from the front (Fig. 23), you can then draw in the outstanding features of the make-up on whichever face applies.

Preparing the Skin

Only a brief look at the different skin types and how to treat them is possible here. There are some very good books (and some very bad ones, too) on the market, and if you are going to work with make-up at all seriously, it's important to give a great deal of attention to the proper care of the different kinds of skin. There are basically six types: normal, dry, oily, acne, combination, and delicate, as described in the following table:

Normal skin	Thin-textured and delicate, soft and with few wrinkles Before applying make-up:	Treat it with a greaseless moisturizer for normal skin during the day, a rich cream at night. Apply a greaseless moisturizing lotion in minimal amounts.
Dry skin	Thin-textured and delicate, with many tiny wrinkles Before applying make-up:	Treat it with a greaseless moisturizing lotion for dry skin; a vegetable non-alcohol-based lotion during the day, a rich cream at night. Apply a greaseless moisturizing cream.
Oily skin	Coarse-textured with large pores, a bit oily on nose, chin, and forehead Before applying make-up:	Treat it with cleansing lotion for oily skin, a greaseless day and night cream, with periodic application of medicated lotion. Nothing needed but a few dabs of medicated lotion, giving a matte finish.

(continued on page 20)

Acne	Similar to oily skin, but with many pimples and blackheads	Treat it by washing often with a sulphur-based soap, with an astringent, greaseless lotion and a cream for day and night.
	Before applying make-up:	Nothing needed but a few dabs of medicated lotion, giving a matte finish.
Combination skin	Some facial areas are oily, others are dry, with pimples and blackheads. The skin is scaly in some areas.	Treat it with chamomile and non-alcohol-based lotion for normal skin, a medium-rich night cream and a greaseless day cream.
	Before applying make-up:	Apply a moisturizing lotion in minimal quantities, or a medicated lotion.
Delicate skin	Thin-textured and delicate, very sensitive to cold and heat. It reddens easily, mostly on the cheeks.	Its care requires a greaseless moisturizing lotion, very rich and nourishing day and night cream.
	Before applying make-up:	Use a nourishing greaseless or medicated lotion.

Lighting

All make-up artists must test out the colors of the products they use under lights, to avoid unexpected problems. In fact, it often happens in film production that even if your make-up is exactly the same for the second time, the lighting may have changed!

Every lighting technician has his or her own priorities and systems. It may be necessary to consult with the lighting director, the cameraman, the camera operator, or, in the case of a photo session, the photographer—in order to get a quick shot of the work you've just done.

Any kind of make-up can be washed out or strengthened by reflected light or changed by the color of it (Fig. 24). When the intensity of the light is decreased, softer reflections result in the room and therefore to the make-up. When the intensity increases, the merits and blemishes show all the more. If materials or clothes absorb or reflect light, avoid particularly emphatic or light make-ups and you'll avoid many unnecessary complications.

> **Remember:**
> Reflected light softens features.
> Porous and dull materials (such as velours) absorb a great deal of light and tone down the make-up.
> Clear and glossy materials (such as sequins) reflect excessive light.

When you do make-up for film productions, you can get more precise results with color than you can in television, where lights and shadows are not so well controlled, due to completely different techniques of lighting and shooting the scene. But, a good lighting technician can get excellent results in either medium, whatever the materials used.

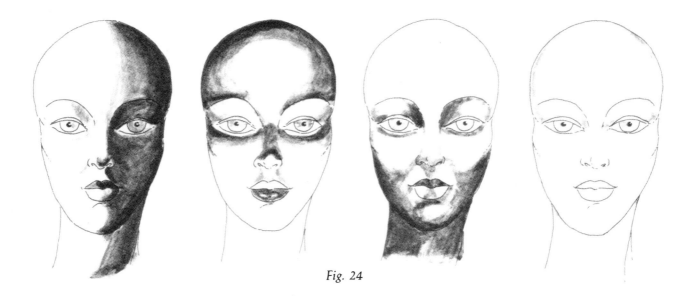

Fig. 24

You'll get more dramatic results with less effort when you work in television than in films. This is because the screen is much smaller, and the picture more concentrated. Every make-up artist working in color video has to avoid heavy and bright shades, intense black and pure white tones, sparkling objects and exaggerated effects, unless required by the script. It's particularly important to avoid all blue and violet tones and their derivatives. I've seen eyes made up in black become enormous dark spots; light layers of blush become harsh and coarse; false eyelashes take over the whole make-up job. I've seen pearly paste eye shadow brighten the face grotesquely; turquoise and intense green eye shadow destroy a refined overall effect; strong-colored wigs appear in extremely bad taste—and it's all been in professional work. You'll avoid many of these pitfalls if you choose appropriate colors that are natural to a particular face.

Remember:
Color video usually requires greater light than black and white does, so the make-up you design will appear more obvious.

If you're working on make-up for television and can't find the right colors among the shades in your make-up kit, you can put several tints together and blend them. Using the primary colors—pure blue, pure yellow, pure red, plus pure white and black—you can arrive at any shade you want. By mixing yellow and blue, you can get all the intermediate tones of green; with red and blue you get the violet tones; red and yellow give you oranges; red and white, the pink shades; red and green, the browns; black and white, the greys; white and blue, the azure tones. This, of course, will be familiar to you if you've done any painting, and that's one of the reasons why the make-up artist needs that basic knowledge, as discussed before. With it, you can handle many situations with ease.

For color video, your choice of foundation make-up will have an effect on every shade of beige being covered.

Without make-up, skin takes on an orange or rose tint. A suntanned person will look quite brown.

To apply make-up on some body areas, use foundation (in tube form) diluted with a greaseless moisturizer. Mix and apply the liquid with a natural sponge.

When you choose a base make-up color for the face, try to stay close to the person's own skin tone. If the subject's complexion is very light, you may want to use a slightly darker foundation; for dark skins, a slightly lighter color.

The best powder to use is the translucent kind, because it doesn't stain or change the color of the make-up.

Remember:
When working in color video or films:
Always use deep browns to darken eyes—even if the person's eyes are black.
Use dark brown, too, and mascara, and blushes derived from soft browns. In any case, avoid reds unless, of course, you want to give the person an extremely healthy, ruddy look.

Choose shades that match the person's hair or wig and won't clash with their costumes and accessories. All the colors used should blend tastefully together.

Make up neck, ears, and lips with the same base color you use for the face, but apply it more sparingly.

With regard to grey hair wigs, hairpieces, sideburns, beards, moustaches, and eyebrows: these can change tone very unexpectedly and produce quite unpleasant effects! For this reason, be extremely careful when you apply grey coloring to the hair of any character. Keep checking and be ready to correct the color, darkening it or lightening it as needed. Always avoid shades of blue-greenish grey, white, and violet or lilac tints. And be sure always to check hairpieces through the movie or the television camera, whatever their color and/or style of manufacture.

Make-Up Techniques

Let's take a quick look at each one of the steps in the make-up process, especially as they apply to motion pictures and television.

Highlighting

Highlighting is almost always done using a shade that ranges from beige to orange, depending on the basic color of the make-up. It can be of the same tone as the foundation but more intense—it can be a slightly different shade. You need to apply it on all the shadowed areas, on such imperfections as pockmarks and scars, and on any parts you wish to enhance.

Follow the four steps listed here for highlighting:

1. Apply a light coat of clear cream stick make-up on the area under the eye, blending the color outwards all the way to the lashes of the lower eyelids.

2. Using the same color, apply the make-up to the folds at the sides of the nose and mouth (Fig. 25).

3. To cover pockmarks or scars, use the same color, blending it carefully.

4. Finally, blend the same color on any sunken areas or on the areas you wish to emphasize.

If the arches of the eyebrows are not very wide and you want to enlarge the eye area, blend a small amount of the light color in this area as well. This highlighting technique is also used when eyes are too close together, to create the look of a longer, straighter line when the nose is too up-turned, to bring out a deep-set chin and jawline, and to heighten a low forehead.

In Fig. 25 the shaded areas show the areas that need to be highlighted. The ones outlined with the dotted lines are optional.

Apply the highlights with a #12 brush or with a small thin rubber sponge. Use only a small amount at a time, blend it carefully and, immediately afterward, pat on a thin coat of translucent powder over the made-up area.

Base Color

Using a thin rubber sponge, take a small amount of foundation and dot it under the eyes where you've already blended in the highlight color. Also dot it on the nose, the lips, and in the center of the chin and forehead. Spread it outward in gentle strokes until you've covered the entire face. Be careful not to get it into the hair.

Now apply another light coat of base, but not too heavily. Spread it over the neck all the way to the edge of the costume and over the ears, decreasing the make-up as you go.

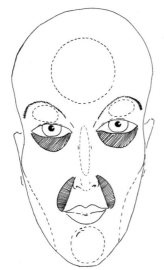

Fig. 25

Shadows

Shadows downplay areas where defects are obvious and minimize overly prominent bones and flesh. You can use them to "correct" far-apart eyes, to tone down cheekbones or a jawline that juts too far forward (never do it on rounded cheeks), to "narrow" very wide faces, de-emphasize crooked noses, soften hard outlines, "pull in" prominent eyebrows, shorten long chins, lower foreheads and minimize double chins (Fig. 26).

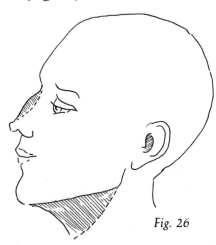

Fig. 26

Use any shade ranging from warm to greyish brown. Blend with a #12 brush to obtain the most natural effect. Fig. 27 shows the areas that generally need to be shaded.

Powder

Applying powder is often one of the most carelessly handled operations in the make-up process, but it's vitally important to do it correctly if you want good results. Every make-up artist uses translucent powder for most purposes. Use colored powder only when you want to create a special effect.

The best way to apply powder is with a velour puff (Fig. 28). Dip the puff into the powder, pat a little on the palm of your hand, shake it and then gently pat it, without rubbing, under the eyes, on the nose, lips, chin, cheeks and forehead, moving from the middle of the face towards the outside.

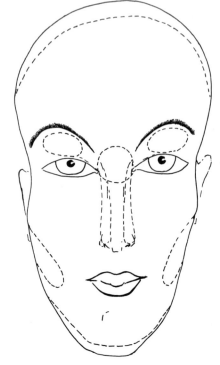

Fig. 27

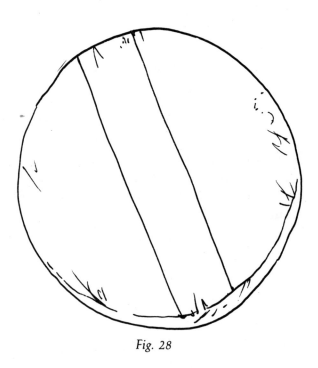

Fig. 28

Remember:
Always use a thin layer of powder on highlighted areas immediately after you apply the light cream stick to set the color and eliminate greasiness.

If the powder container has a plastic covering, don't remove it: it's better to poke holes in the material with a straight pin, which allows the powder to come out easily but keeps it from flying all over when you open the box (Fig. 29). Of course, a small amount of powder will escape inside the cover every time you turn the box upside down, but it won't create the mess that a completely spilled box of powder will.

To test the quality of a translucent powder, put a pinch of it in a cup containing a few teaspoons of petroleum jelly. Stir it. If the mixture turns a light color, the powder is translucent. If it's dark, you've got a colored powder.

Fig. 29

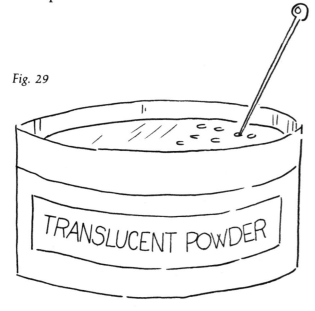

Eyes

You can make up eyes in dozens of ways, but here we'll look at the types of eye make-up most frequently used in theatre, films, television, fashion photography, and in everyday life.

Eye shadow is available in a variety of forms:
- loose powder (in a compact)
- pencil
- cream
- liquid
- stick

For our purposes, the best kinds are the water-soluble or powdered ones, which come in cake form. You can add water or apply them dry.

To spread them on the eyelids, you can use several different sizes of brushes, from #0 to #8 or—even better—sponge applicators. If you're using a water-soluble product, it's a good idea to apply another layer of powdered eye shadow on top of it to emphasize the eye and make the color more vivid.

Remember:
Avoid stick and cream eye shadows. They smudge easily and leave lines that are difficult to blend.
Don't use eye shadow on oily or greasy lids. Always powder the lids lightly before you apply eye shadow of any type.
Eyeliner pencils are easy to use and the lines can be blended perfectly. They shouldn't be too soft, if you want the line to last for any length of time.

Bascially, there are three sizes of eyes for which you will be doing make-up: small, average, and almond-shaped eyes. Small eyes must be enlarged or widened if they are too round. Average eyes require no size correction. Almond-shaped eyes must be corrected if they are too close together or set too deeply in the face.

Small Eyes (Figs. 30–32)
Use water-soluble eye shadow and deep brown eyeliner or brown pencil.

1. Draw a line near the upper eyelashes with the pencil or with a #0 brush, from the center of the eye (A) to the outside crease of the lid.

2. Draw a line under the eye, starting about one-quarter of the distance from the inside corner (B).

3. Make the lower line reach the upper one as well as the line which will be drawn on the crease of the lid (C).

Leave an empty corner outside the eye itself, as shown in Figs. 30 and 31.

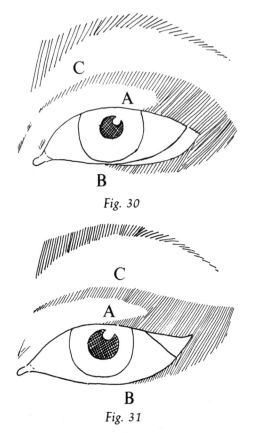

Fig. 30

Fig. 31

4. Blend the color together with marten brushes #3, #5, and #8.

Generally, the above sort of make-up requires false eyelashes, applied in tufts. Attach them along the contour of the eye all the way to the end of the false outside corner (Fig. 32).

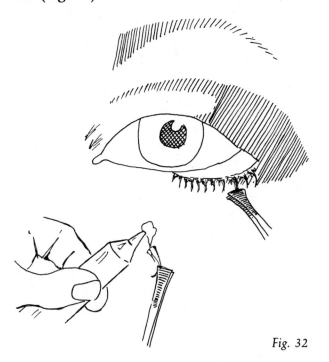

Fig. 32

Average Eyes (Figs. 33–34)

Do make-up for average-sized eyes in the same way, but avoid the artificial corner and draw only lines (A) and (B), bordering the eye until they join together on the lid at the true outside corner.

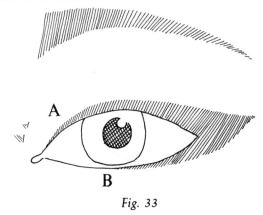

Fig. 33

The same version, with the dark line on the crease of the lid (Fig. 34), helps to enlarge eyes with very widely arched eyebrows.

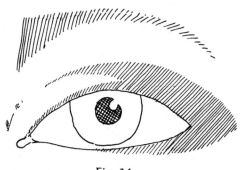

Fig. 34

Almond-shaped Eyes (Fig. 35)

Use a light eye shadow on the lid. With a pencil, eyeliner, or a dark water-soluble eye shadow, create an outline that forms a "U"—from the inside corner of the crease of the lid (A), and from a point one-quarter of the way underneath the eye (B).

Darken the outer corner slightly (C) and blend with brushes #3, #5, and #8.

Choosing the color of the eye shadow is a personal matter and depends on the shape of the eye and its color, as well as upon hair color and costume. Just keep in mind that light colors stand out and dark ones recede, and then select the shade that suits your purpose.

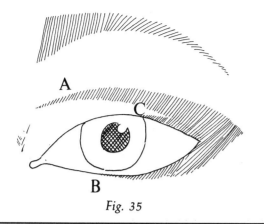

Fig. 35

> **Remember:**
> Extremely pearly eye shadow (unless you're using it for fashion photography) should be avoided, as it gives a metallic, smudgy look.
>
> When black—or any other dark shade—is used on the eyelid, it does, of course, give a deeper and more intense look, but it also makes the eyes look considerably smaller.
>
> A dark beige or cinnamon color on the same area enlarges the eyes and gives an attractive look.

Some time ago, eyeliner was commonly used to outline the eyes above and below, ending with "wings." The line was usually drawn in a hard, precise way that, even if it helped to make the eyes look larger, gave them a cold expression. You can use this technique if you like, but generally it's a better idea to draw only a very thin line and then blend it with a brush. If you're working on a production that calls for this kind of make-up (it was very popular in the 1960s), use it, by all means, but select an eyeliner that blends easily with marten brush #4.

Eyebrows

Always shape eyebrows in a way that suits the subject's face—not just the dictates of fashion. Make them an appropriate thickness and neither too long nor too short.

Before plucking the eyebrows to remove unwanted hairs, carefully draw in both eyebrows with an eyebrow pencil till they look just the way you want them. Then you can see where you need to work, and avoid plucking hairs which will actually contribute to the well-shaped eyebrow line.

When you correct the eyebrows this way, use pencils of the same hair color or of a slightly darker shade, for example:

Hair color	Pencil color
Black	very dark brown
Blond	amber or honey
Brown	light brown
Red	reddish brown
Grey	medium grey
White	light grey

For completely plucked eyebrows, the same technique is fine, but use a #0 brush dipped in liquid eyeliner of a suitable color. Stroke in the eyebrows carefully, hair by hair, in order to make them appear as natural as possible. It's a good idea to sketch the shape in lightly first (Fig. 36), then proceed with the stroking motions (Fig. 37).

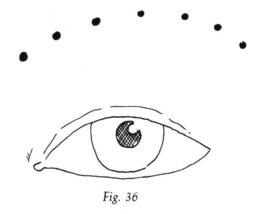

Fig. 36

When you draw in the shape of the eyebrow, don't close the arch over both sides of the eye. Keep the eyebrows at a level where they will contribute to the natural line of the eye. If you make them too low or too high, you may get a satanic look (Fig. 38).

Look at Fig. 39 for some ideas for eyebrow shapes with different characteristics.

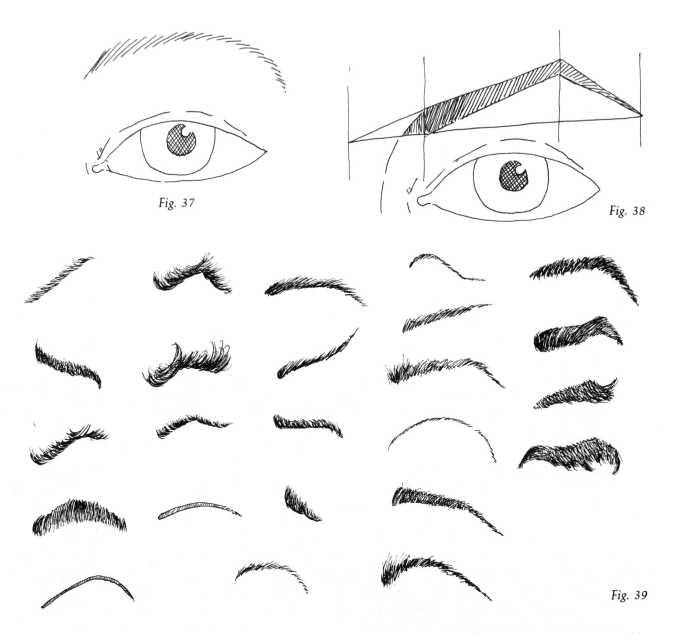

Fig. 37

Fig. 38

Fig. 39

Mascara

Mascara is available in various styles: paste, compact, or cream form. You can get mascaras in tubes to apply with a dry brush. Those in cake form need to be applied with a moistened brush, and those in stick form come with a roll-on wand and a small brush. They also come in various colors, and you can get them mixed with synthetic powdered fibres that lengthen the eyelashes as you apply them.

The best mascara for professional use is the wand type in fairly dark colors. Bright colors, as we've already seen, produce showy effects that are better used for imagi-native or special-effects make-ups. Use dark brown mascara for people with blond, red, or light brown hair; black mascara for black or dark brown hair; and very dark grey for grey or white hair.

Let's say you're using mascara from a tube. Squeeze a tiny amount of cream on the back of your hand, and then apply a thin coat of it on the eyelashes, using the brush horizontally first and then vertically, starting from the root. If you pull the lid gently towards the outer corner of the eye, with your fingers, you'll get the lashes to separate from each other (Fig. 40) and it should be easier to apply the mascara evenly.

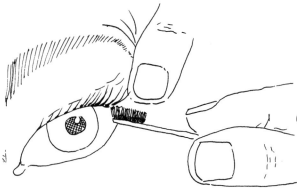

Fig. 40

If the eyelashes are not very curly or if they're droopy, you may want to use an eyelash curler on them (Fig. 41). Do it before you apply the mascara. If you do it afterwards, you'll end up with sticky eyelashes and a dirty eyelash curler. Be sure the tool has soft rubber protectors on it, and use it carefully. Always keep the eyelash curler clean. After you use it, disinfect it with alcohol.

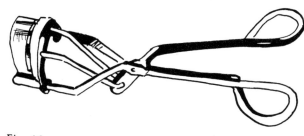

Fig. 41

There's no rule about which eyelashes to begin with in applying mascara. Some make-up artists (I am among them) apply it to the lower lashes first and then to the upper ones. Others do just the opposite and get the same result. Decide for yourself how you want to do it.

If you smudge make-up in the eye area, you can remove it by dipping a cotton ball in a non-oily make-up remover and gently dabbing the smudged area.

False Eyelashes

False eyelashes are available in many different forms, from the most natural-looking to the most artificial. Choose eyelashes that have a natural curl, are not too long,

and are attached to a thin, plastic thread rather than to a very visible tape. Lashes in tufts—or even singly—look more natural and are easier to attach than the fully prepared ones, though they take longer to apply. Keep the following steps in mind when applying false eyelashes.

1. First, with a water-based eye shadow, darken the area on which the false lash will be attached.

2. With tweezers, pick up the lashes and, holding them at the side, apply a layer of eyelash adhesive on the part that will be attached to the lid (Figs. 42 and 43).

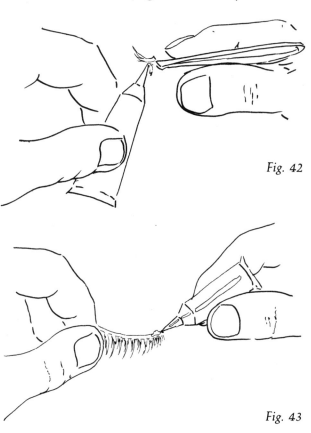

Fig. 42

Fig. 43

3. Apply the false eyelashes as closely as possible to the base of the real lashes, pressing gently with the back of the tweezers (Fig. 44). Don't put them too near the inner or outer corner of the eye. If you do, they are likely to come off as the eye opens and closes.

4. Make the lashes thickest towards the outside of the lid (Fig. 45).

5. If the real lashes are much shorter than the false ones, apply a thin coat of mascara

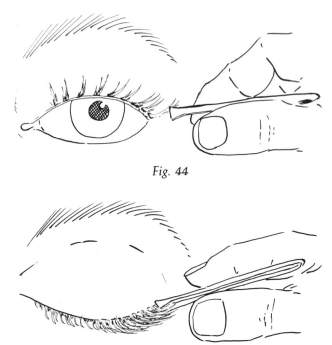

Fig. 44

Fig. 45

to the ends of the real lashes. Then, pressing with the back of the tweezers and using your fingers, attach them to the false ones.

6. If the adhesive that holds the lashes on is too obvious, touch it up using a water-soluble eye shadow applied with a thin brush.

You don't need to use mascara on false lashes. They are already very dark and bright.

You can use the same method to attach eyelashes in tufts that you use with those on tape, with one difference: When you work with the tufts, you need to stretch the lid outwards slightly with your fingers. Apply the tufts fairly close together.

Eyelashes made with single hairs must be attached near the root of the real lashes. In any case use the white adhesive that is made for this purpose and becomes transparent when it dries.

If you wish to color the adhesive black, mix it with a small amount of mascara before it dries.

To clean false eyelashes, first remove them and wipe off the excess dry adhesive with your fingers. Then clean the hairline with a little brush dipped in acetone, and finally go over the hairs with a liquid make-

up remover. Finally, rinse with water so they will be ready for use.

Blush

Blush is available in many forms: powder, cake or stick, flat or pearly. Avoid those in powder or stick form and also the pearly variety. Powder blushes are difficult to work with. If you use too much, the cheeks look stained and overdone. The stick form is appropriate only for certain kinds of skin—for the dry and wrinkled skins of elderly people, for example—and it requires more time to blend. Both of them often smudge on the skin. Pearly blush creates artificial-looking effects.

Cake blush is the best type to use, preferably in an amber shade, similar to the color of a natural, healthy glow. Use only a minimal amount because it can be really difficult to remove excess color once it's on. Use large, very soft brushes that are gripped firmly by the handle, so the bristles don't come off all over the subject's face.

These cake—or compact—blushes are also the easiest type of blush to remove: You can do it with a brush and it takes very little time, which is always precious in this work.

We use color on the cheeks only to highlight the shade of the overall skin tone, and not to make the subject look unusual. The amount of blush to use depends on the dictates of fashion, and the only real rule of thumb is to use it in shades and quantities which complement the make-up. Never allow yourself to get too tied to fashion. Never be too extreme. Only when you're using make-up to emphasize specific characteristics—or on such characters as farmers, whose skin needs to look sunburned—should you apply an excessive amount of blush.

Lips

Sometimes, before applying lipstick, it helps to outline the lips with a pencil. Perfect lips rarely need to be outlined, unless you want to emphasize them for some reason. But you may want to "correct" lips that are less than perfect. For a useful, illustrated plan for lip corrections and outlining techniques, see Figs. 46 and 47.

In any case, before using lipstick, lightly coat the lips with foundation and dry them by applying a thin layer of translucent

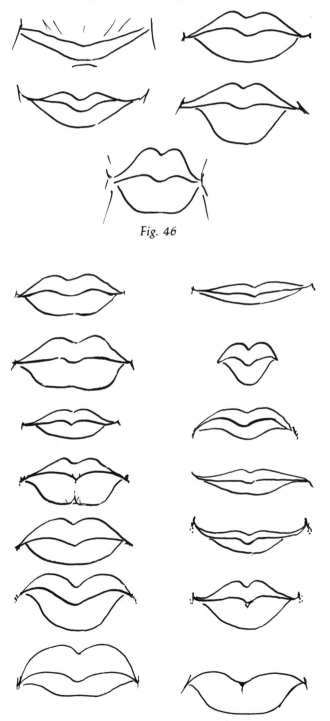

Fig. 46

Fig. 47

powder. Then outline them, using a pencil darker than the lipstick color, drawing a light line from the outside towards the inside for the lower lip and from the inside towards the outside for the upper lip (Fig. 48). Keep the line extremely thin towards the outer corners of the mouth. The pencil outline filled in with lipstick will give longer-lasting results, because the lead of the pencil, made of wax and pigment, keeps the lips waterproof.

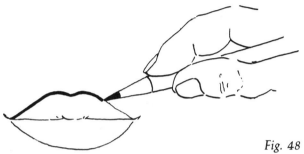

Fig. 48

To correct pencil smudges and get a finer outline, spread foundation (in the same shade used for the face) over the outline of the lips with a #3 brush and then powder the area. Finally, with brush #4, apply the lipstick, following the same procedure for the outline, always taking care to keep the lipstick within the outlines, especially at the outer corners of the lips. Never choose an overly hard or soft pencil or one that is difficult to remove.

Use lipsticks that are specially prepared for film and video work; other types will smear immediately after you apply them. For best results, use a minimal amount of lipstick. It's always easier to add than subtract!

If you have to brighten lips, apply a very thin coat of gloss. Lip gloss has to be almost transparent. If the pencil outline of the lip smears, touch up the area with the foundation you're using for the rest of the face, applied with a #3 or #4 brush. Then, with another thin brush, apply some powder.

Remove excess lipstick by blotting with a tissue between the upper and lower lips.

Always avoid using bright or dark red lipstick on very full lips or on those with a particularly unusual shape. For these kinds of lips, select a medium–color lipstick—and a light gloss. In Figs. 49 and 50, you'll see a number of types of lips with a possible pencil-outline correction. The corrections are shown in the dotted lines.

To clean lipstick brushes: Dip them in alcohol for a few minutes, then wash with water and shampoo.

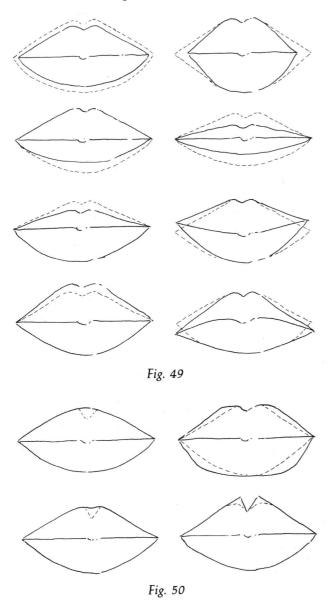

Fig. 49

Fig. 50

Removing Hair

When body hair needs to be removed, it's always advisable to have it done by an experienced beautician, using the warm-wax method of depilation. However, for a few stray hairs or facial hair, a depilatory

cream may be better (some excellent ones are available). Most of them are left on the face for about ten minutes and then removed with tepid water. Remember though, that for at least half an hour you have to avoid using creams or lotions on the treated area.

Dyeing Lashes and Brows

If lashes and eyebrows need to be dyed, go to an expert who can do it safely, quickly and well. As far as color is concerned, keep in mind the suggestions on page 27, for relating eyebrow color to the hair. Avoid, for example, giving an aged, white-haired character black eyebrows! The overall color scheme of hair, face, and costume should be complementary and match perfectly.

Dyeing Hair

To change hair color, you may want to use hair sprays or pomades that do the job temporarily. They are available in various colors. This type of procedure may be all right in theatre or in an emergency, but if you're working in films or television, get the help of a good hairstylist, who knows how to work with every kind of hair and achieve the color effects you want.

Tan

To get a natural-looking body tan, you can choose among four methods listed below. First of all, be sure to select a natural-looking color—golden bronze, or close to it—avoiding yellowish or greyish tones.

1. Using cake make-up and a big, damp natural sponge, apply the make-up to areas of your body, hands, and face where you want the tan (Fig. 51).

To give the illusion of gleaming, tanned skin, spray some brilliantine over the particular area from two to three inches away or as stated on the can (Fig. 52).

2. Another tanning trick which is un-

brown powder (Fig. 53) to create the glossy, tanned effect, in the following proportions:

20 percent powder
20 percent isopropyl alcohol
60 percent glycerine

Apply the mixture on face and body with a natural sponge moistened in any alcohol-based lotion or in diluted isopropyl alcohol. This technique is highly successful.

Fig. 53

4. The last method is decidedly more difficult than the others. It seems quite easy, but if you don't get it exactly right, you won't get satisfactory results. Spread a moisturizing non-oily cream over face and body (Fig. 54). Take a small amount of oil-based foundation make-up, mixed with a lot of brown powder and massage it quickly on the area to be "tanned" (Fig. 55).

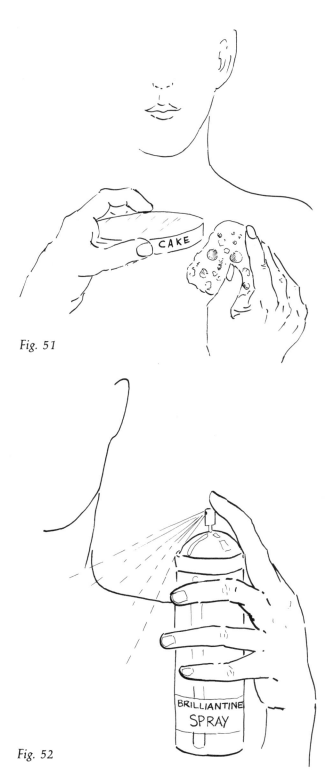

Fig. 51

Fig. 52

doubtedly effective is to use cake make-up mixed with flesh-colored glitter. The procedure is the same as in the first method, but skips the brilliantine. The glitter itself produces the effect of a gleaming, tanned body.

3. In Hollywood, make-up artists use a mixture of glycerine, isopropyl alcohol, and

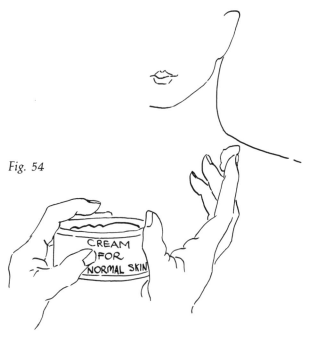

Fig. 54

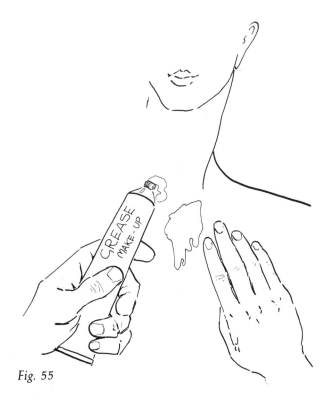

Fig. 55

With a sponge moistened in an alcohol-based lotion, spread the foundation until it's completely absorbed and perfectly blended (Fig. 56).

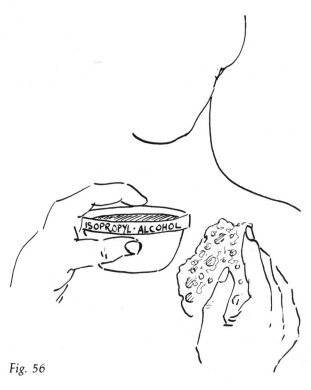

Fig. 56

Any of the methods listed above will need special care, especially when you're making up your hands and feet or other body areas.

Once your body is made up, avoid getting wet. Even the smallest quantity of water can produce streaks or smudges that are difficult to correct. Obviously, after tanning yourself by using any of these methods, you're not going to be able to enjoy much action in the pool! But as long as you stay out of the water, the results will be good.

For longer and more complicated scenes—where you have to get wet—you'll need to apply an artificial tanning cream the night before. Be sure to use waterproof eye shadow and waterproof mascara, too! Generally, when you're trying to get a tanned-face effect, you can skip highlighting and shadowing. These are not at all useful for a tanned look.

Make-up for Dark Skin

Use little foundation make-up, unless there are many blemishes. Otherwise the look will be heavy and unreal.

Choose a foundation that matches the skin tone of the person you're making up.

On areas to be hollowed out, use dark brown shades. Highlight and shadow in amber tones that verge on bronze-orange.

Choose eye shadow colors that show up on dark skin. Blend them carefully so that you don't create obvious outlines and a made-up look.

A few possible eye-shadow shades are purple, orange, pinkish gold, bronze, peacock blue, emerald green.

Use black for the outline of eyes, lashes, and brows (see hair color rules on page 27). False eyelashes need to be black.

For lips and cheeks, use all rosy tones: orange, lilac, coral, fuchsia, cherry red, and vermilion, except on excessively full lips, which require only a bit of translucent gloss.

Use grey shades only on grey-haired people. False eyelashes in this case will have to be lighter.

Make-up for Yellow Skin

When making up oriental subjects, use rosy or coral foundation. Don't try to make up the eyes to look European, but create highlights and shadows with brown tones, and you'll get excellent results.

Fashion Photography

All the rules you learned for film and television make-up hold for natural-type fashion photography. Of course, if you want an ultrasophisticated effect, you can create a dramatic make-up that would be unbelievable and rather ghastly on film, but may be suggestive and even inspired for the fashion pages.

Make-up for Young People

Generally, don't use foundation make-up on children and teenagers, or you'll create false, doll-like faces.

Use only a little blush on the cheeks to lighten up particularly pale complexions and a touch of lip gloss over a thin coat of lip rouge.

Make-up for Bearded Subjects

It's a good idea to keep a razor or electric shaver for those people who come to the make-up room with unshaven beards. If the shadow of the beard remains visible even after the shave, and after you spread the foundation, apply a very thin coating of amber-colored base to cover the blue shadow. Greasepaint is just as good for this purpose as a heavy foundation. In any case, remember that the *total* absence of this shadow sometimes gives the character a false, manikinlike look.

Make-up for Special Effects

There are no precise rules for spectacular effects and imaginative make-up. Everything depends on the originality and inspiration of the specific make-up artist.

Almost always, before work starts on any film, television, or theatre piece, the technicians and directors meet to exchange ideas, plans, and schedules. The make-up artist needs to be in close contact with them and with the director, who generally, in the end, decides everything.

It's also a good idea for make-up artists to set up appointments with the actors well ahead of time. While a make-up job will take about fifteen minutes, if it's simple and the character is not particularly important, it may take an hour for those with more detailed make-ups and from two to seven or even eight hours for elaborate make-ups or those that call for major transformations: advanced age, illness, etc. It's important to have good photographic material for reference. Read the script and gather the photos and other information you'll need. Collect data on the "look" or the make-up of the period in history if that is involved.

If an actor is playing the part of a famous person, it's essential to get as much information as you can about the character, along with photos and paintings to keep handy for quick reference.

Always make an appointment with the stage manager or the assistants who alert the actors to report to the make-up room. Remember that when you're working in films, you'll need extra time to get the make-up right. The screen enlarges the images so fantastically that they require all the care and attention you can lavish on them.

Tell women to come to the make-up room with clean faces and men to come already shaved, in order to save time.

Take photographs of all the made-up characters, facing front and in profile, and keep the ones that may be useful to you in the future.

Go to the set yourself, or get one of your assistants to go, and keep an eye on the actors after they're made up, so you can fix them up if the job is spoiled or smeared. Pay particular attention to false pieces (noses, ears, pot bellies, etc.), because these are very sensitive to perspiration and are apt to collapse under lights and in high temperatures.

Every night, clean everything in your make-up kit that is dirty. Above all, keep the net edges of wigs and hairpieces clean.

Age Make-up

If you have to make up actors to look middle-aged or older, read the script! Are the characters healthy or sick? Have they been exposed to sunlight during their entire lives or do they hibernate in a city high-rise or a musty office? Certainly, you don't have to develop an individual make-up type for every kind of profession or activity, but skilled make-up artists will be aware of these differences. They will automatically analyze the faces of the people they meet in everyday life—in the street, in shops, in offices, on buses and planes, outdoors— identify the shades and skin tones that characterize them, and put these valuable insights to work at the right moment.

Ages 40–50

For the make-up foundation, you'll need a product that's a couple of tones lighter than the skin color of the actor you're making up.

For shadows, use a foundation that is two shades darker than the base. For deep hollows, choose a medium greyish brown and blend it carefully with the help of #8 and #12 brushes. You'll want to apply it on all rounded areas, on temples, along the lines that run from nose to mouth, and at the sides of the mouth.

Never leave lines unblended, as this gives a "painted" look to the face. That kind of make-up will be suitable for slim people with thin features and slender bones. But for sturdy and fat people, such fatty areas as jowls and double chins need to be enhanced with a light foundation. Use

darker shadows on the hollows around them for emphasis.

Another way to do a middle-aged make-up is to avoid making up the face at all— leaving it completely natural—adding only a few faded shadows, a little white on the hair at the temples and a few on the brows, if the subject is male. For older women also, an unmade-up face with dark shadows, an appropriate hairstyle and hair color along with slightly plucked eyebrows, gives a very believable older look.

Since this system requires no foundation, if you want to add age marks or show advancing age, just moisten your brush in castor oil, dip it into the chosen color, and apply it directly to the face. You'll need to powder afterward.

If you're working on a film, you may want to use one of the adhesive products that creates convincing-looking wrinkles, but first draw in the lines and shaded areas the older face should have (Fig. 57). If you wait until after the aging paste is on, you'll have trouble blending the lines and shadows and the general effect will not be so good. (More about the aging paste on page 102.)

To create the hollow cheeks and flabby skin, see Fig. 58. First draw the fold onto the face with a brown pencil (A). Then immediately next to it and above it, draw a reddish line (B). Underneath the brown line (A) draw a light beige line (C), and then blend the edges of the color with #4, #8, and #12 brushes.

The reddish color creates a deep and realistic-looking shadow, while the light beige area highlights the flabby muscle. The overall effect is quite believable. A good way to add years to an already aged male make-up is to add a grizzled beard or moustache.

Ages 60–70

It's easy to achieve the look of this age for work in the theatre: Very strong shadows and highlights are sufficient. But if

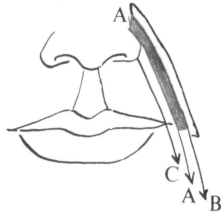

Fig. 58

you're working in films or television, you may need to add layers of aging glue or paste—or even artificial latex parts (such as caps, to get the effect of baldness), or other pieces that give the impression of loose jowls, flabby muscles, and so on.

You may want to make up both hair and eyebrows with an orange-beige color in liquid or cake form. This color will help avoid the bluish halo that appears if you apply pure white to the hair.

Every area to be shadowed should be faded using a dark tone, while the base color should be three shades lighter than the natural skin tone.

Lips should look paler than the skin and approach a yellowish or bluish shade.

To give a flabby look when you're working for television, you might use netting to indicate the sagging of some muscles or some other areas. More about the use of netting on page 39. For films, though, you'll need to employ artificial parts, especially on rounded areas.

For older women, you may want to add a light-colored wig, one that is appropriate to the age and personality of the character.

And for any work in films, if you want a very believable image, get hair and eyebrows colored by a good beautician.

When aging the hands, indicate the sunken and prominent areas with appropriate foundation, highlights, and shadow, emphasizing the bony parts. Then apply a couple of layers of aging glue and stress the veins with a bluish color.

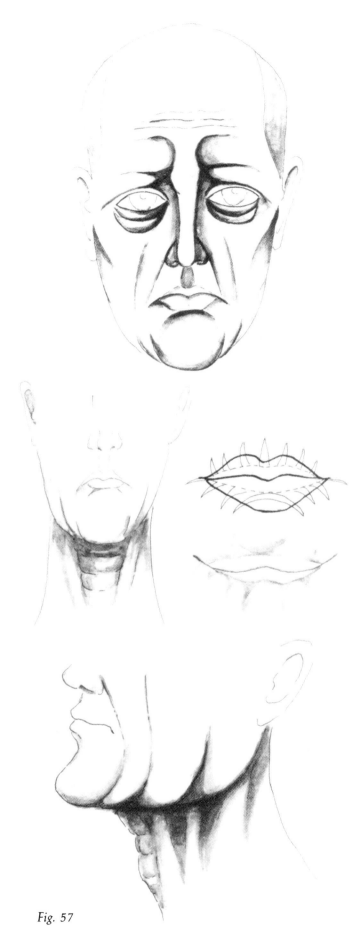

Fig. 57

37

Ages 80-90-100

If you use artificial pieces of aging paste, you'll need two assistants: one to dry the aging product that you apply and another to hold the skin taut of the person to be made up.

You can get a very obvious wrinkling of the skin with cotton and latex or facial tissues and latex (more about how to do it later on). Perhaps the most successful method is to work with foam latex parts, such as a cap with sparse hair or none at all.

Shading on the face should be hard, highlights and shadows more accentuated, hands made up in a "stressed" way.

Warning:
If you're working in a production where the character ages through different scenes—or gets younger in flashbacks —you may have to make these changes in a very short time. Be very careful about anything you add or remove to change the appearance at different ages; it's very easy to make mistakes. Don't let yourself feel rushed or panicked. Besides changing highlights and shadows, it's quickest and easiest to change hairstyle or wig, to add or remove moustache and beard.

Making Actors Look Younger

To remove years from a wrinkled face with flabby muscles and typically pale, greyish skin, you'll need to use a foundation two or three shades darker than the actor's natural complexion. Apply it with a thin rubber sponge. Blend all the fatty, sagging areas, such as double chin or jowls, with a dark color verging on brown.

Male characters' eyebrows may need to be plucked, females' filled up and darkened. Lashes should be dark. If they are not full, thicken them by applying false lashes one at a time.

Highlight grey areas with a color three shades lighter than that of the natural skin. Bags under the eyes should be shadowed.

Select a youthful hairstyle. If the hair is grey, color it in some way. You may want to use a wig or hairpiece to make the character appear younger.

Beards and moustaches should be trimmed neatly or shaved off.

Making Lifts

If the actor has a double chin or flabby muscles, some "lifts" may be required, devices that lift and smooth out baggy skin.

The best way to apply lifts is to cut strips from 100 percent silk fabric—four inches long by two-thirds of an inch wide. Make two triangular cuts—one on either side of the upper section—as in Fig. 59. Cut a substantial length of surgical thread. Ideally, the strips and thread should be the same hair color of the person being made up. Spread a strong adhesive at the top of the silk strip and attach the thread to it as illustrated so that it's the same length on either side of the strip. Then fold the strip at the line of the triangular cuts, so that it sticks together. When the strip is dry, apply the lift to the face with a strong adhesive wherever you want to lift a flabby area. The part with the stretched-out thread should be turned upwards. At this point, knot the thread so that it forms little rings for the length that you need (see Fig. 59), and snip off the excess thread.

If you make a lift such as this for one side of the face, you'll need to make an identical one for the other side.

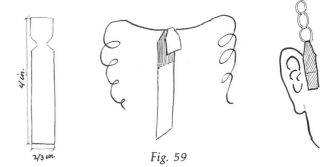

Fig. 59

Next fasten a little hook to the last ring on one side (Fig. 60). Pull the two threads and slip the hook into the ring, pulling up the skin of the face along with it. Don't pull the threads *too* much or you'll create ugly folds near the cheekbone and the ear.

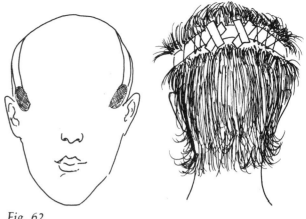

Fig. 62

Fig. 60

Another way to make lifts is to sew some oval-shaped strips of netting—two inches long and three-fourths of an inch wide—onto cotton tapes twelve inches long and three-fourths of an inch wide (see Fig. 61).

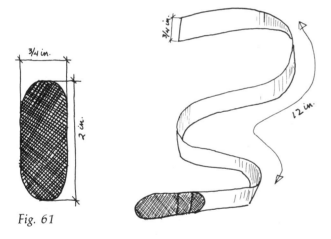

Fig. 61

Attach the netting part to the face with a strong adhesive. Knot the cotton ends together at the back of the head. Fasten this band to the hair with some hairpins.

If you're working with bald people, attach the lifts with strong adhesive on dry areas of the head and neck (Fig. 62). Since the lifts and the support for them are clearly visible, you'll need a very good make-up job to conceal them. Sometimes a few locks of hair or sideburns will do the trick.

There is another—better—way to create lifts, and if you do it well, they'll be almost invisible. This method involves building up layers of soft latex. You'll need a fairly deep ceramic plate or dish, which you turn upside down. Using an ox-bristle brush, paint three oval-shaped latex coats directly onto a section of the plate (Fig. 63). After

Fig. 63

each coat, put the brush in soapy water and dry it, without rinsing. Continue applying coats of latex—as many as ten or twelve applications—gradually diminishing until point C (Fig. 64), where you need to insert a

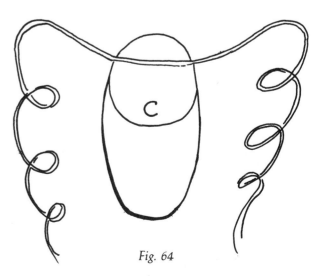

Fig. 64

length of surgical thread, leaving the exact same length on either side. Then knot the thread in rings (as on page 39), and apply a hook to one end.

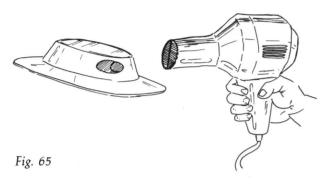

Fig. 65

Dry the latex lift using a hairdryer (Fig. 65), powder it, carefully remove it from the plate, and powder it again. At this point it is ready to use.

Spread a strong adhesive paste on it, wait a minute, and then apply it to the skin (Fig. 66–68).

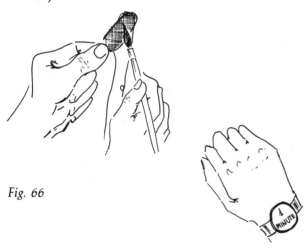

Fig. 66

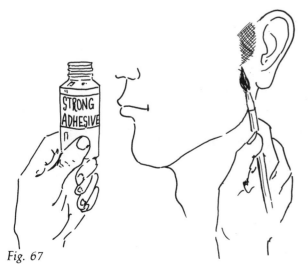

Fig. 67

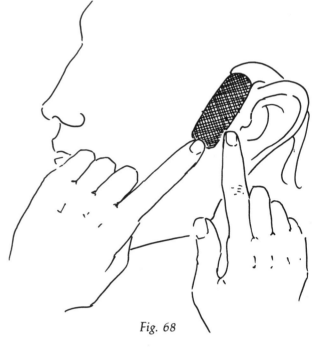

Fig. 68

The part of the lift that incorporates the string is easy to hide in your hair. Next, with a sponge applicator, apply a plastic sealer to the latex lift (Fig. 69). Spread an appropriate foundation base. If it is not heavy enough to cover, use greasepaint (Fig. 70). Then powder abundantly (Fig. 71).

Note that when you use synthetic or silk lifts, foundation is applied *after* the lift goes on the skin. Using the netting method, the face is made up ahead of time and just powdered afterwards.

This method is popular among make-up artists who use it for aging film stars who

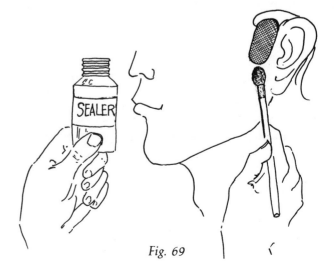

Fig. 69

Another way to make a face look younger is to use a natural lift—such as braids. Start the braids at the hairline, using three thin strands of hair. Braid them neatly and then, with both hands, pull them tight. At the same time, someone else should knot a string around the end of each braid to keep it from unravelling (Fig. 72). Then cross the braids at the back of the head, pin them down, and hide them under other hair.

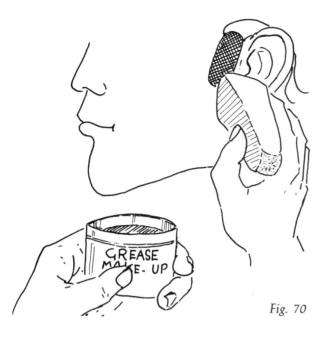

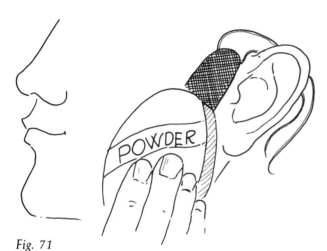

Fig. 70

Fig. 71

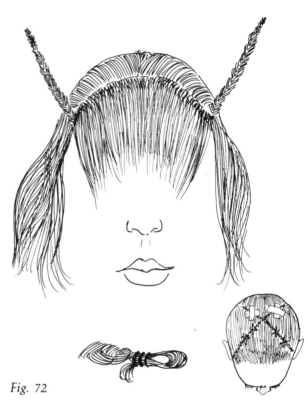

Fig. 72

prefer not wearing a wig and don't want the lifts to show.

Checklist for Rejuvenating an Older Face

1. Highlight
2. Powder
3. Foundation
4. Shadow
5. Eyes
6. Eyebrows
7. Mascara
8. False eyelashes
9. Powder blush
10. Lifts and Touching Up
11. Wigs or Special Hairstyle
12. Lips

For theatre and black-and-white video, it's important to darken grey hair and fill in receding hairlines or blank spaces due to baldness. Use hair color in liquid or cake form, or you can pencil in the hair. For films and color video, it's better to use a hairpiece after you complete the make-up.

Wigs

If you're going to use a wig, it helps to wear a cap made out of a nylon stocking under it to keep the hair in place. Gather the hair in pin curls and keep them firm with crossed pins (Fig. 73). Then fasten a

Fig. 73

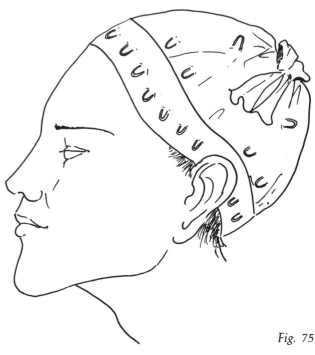

Fig. 75

piece of nylon stocking to your hair, with hairpins inserted first towards the nape of the neck and then towards the face (Fig. 74). Pull the balance of the stocking back, knot it, fasten it with some other hairpins, and you're ready to put on the wig (Fig. 75).

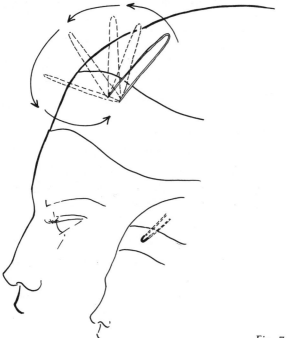

Fig. 74

Make-up for the Stage

Stage make-up doesn't necessarily have to be heavy: Well-done, careful work is often more effective and seems more believable. But no matter how small the theatre is, the audience is always a certain distance away from the stage, and the amount of make-up needed is directly proportional to that distance. The farther away, the more the highlights and shadows need to be emphasized, the eyes enlarged, and the mouth outlined in order for the character's features to be seen. Many of the top make-up artists in films and television learned their craft working in the theatre, so let's take a look at some of those techniques.

First of all, for make-up artists to be successful, they need to have a working knowledge of the expressions and proportions of the human face (Figs. 76–84).

For an ordinary make-up job, select base colors that approximate biscuit tones for men, rosy tones for women. For older people, lean towards greyish-beige colors; for farmers and outdoor types, pick a reddish base. Eyebrows should be emphasized and blush heightened.

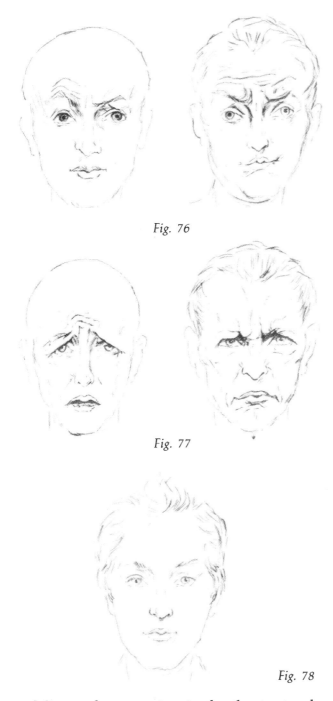

Fig. 76

Fig. 77

Fig. 78

give more expression (Figs. 85 and 86 on page 46). If you're making up women, apply eyelashes on tape (it's more practical and easier), but for men—if they need eyelashes at all—use them in tufts: This looks more natural and is less troublesome.

Select any shade of eye shadow that you wish. Make it as obvious as you want, especially in musical comedy.

If you're doing make-up for ballet dancers, use a light base color and heavy outlines for eyes and brows, which should be lengthened on the ends, stretching upwards towards the temples (Fig. 87).

When you're doing age make-up, spread a light base color, as mentioned before, and draw flabby areas with beige, burgundy, and dark brown shades. Blend these lines, but leave them obvious enough so that they show from a distance.

Powder abundantly, and then apply the wig, if one is going to be used. For theatre, as well as for films, try to get well-made wigs with netting at the hairline.

Apply a thin, rosy, ash-beige layer of base on the brows to absorb light and make up the lips with a bluish shade.

When you need to make temporary and drastic changes in an actor's make-up in the theatre, you'll either want to use putty, which is excellent for making slight alterations to the nose or chin, or some kind of padding or stuffing, which is more successful in making larger changes, such as double chins, protruding foreheads, tummies, bosoms, etc.

One type of padding consists of building up layers of cotton and adhesive over the part in question. The adhesive is the same kind you'd use for beards and moustaches—spirit gum is fine—and after you apply it, add tufts of cotton to it, thicker in the center and thinner at the borders. After each application of adhesive, brush the surface and let it dry completely.

When the padded shape reaches the desired proportions, model it with slightly greasy fingers (so the cotton doesn't stick to them), thinning the edges so that the shape

Most make-up artists in the theatre tend to use cake make-up rather than stick, because it holds better and longer, it's quicker to apply, and it doesn't require powder or any special care during the performance.

Blend all lines—both light and dark—spread the base carefully (in minimal amounts), and put on wigs carefully.

It's always advisable to use false eyelashes for the stage, even if you just rely on them alone, without any additional outlines or emphasis. They will enlarge the eyes and

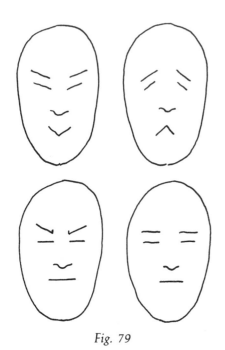

Fig. 79

blends with the person's face or body. Dry with a hairdryer and then, if needed, apply a heavy foundation in a strong color.

Very often, a cap is used to simulate a bald head. For stage purposes, this type of cap doesn't require the thin edge that it does for films, because the ridge won't show from a distance. (More about caps on page 94.)

On page 47, you'll find a chart that shows the changes that make-up undergoes under stage lighting and how to counterbalance it. Since theatrical lighting is generally focused in one direction, or on one area, we can pinpoint each problem clearly. When dealing with films and television, lighting is more indirect, since it has to work for the whole scene.

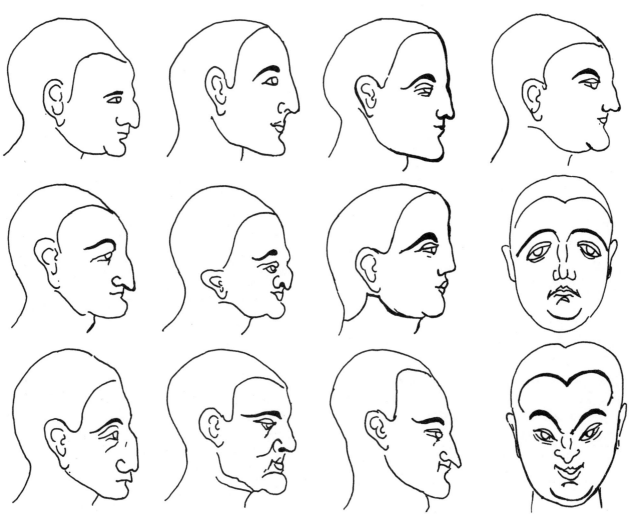

Fig. 80

44

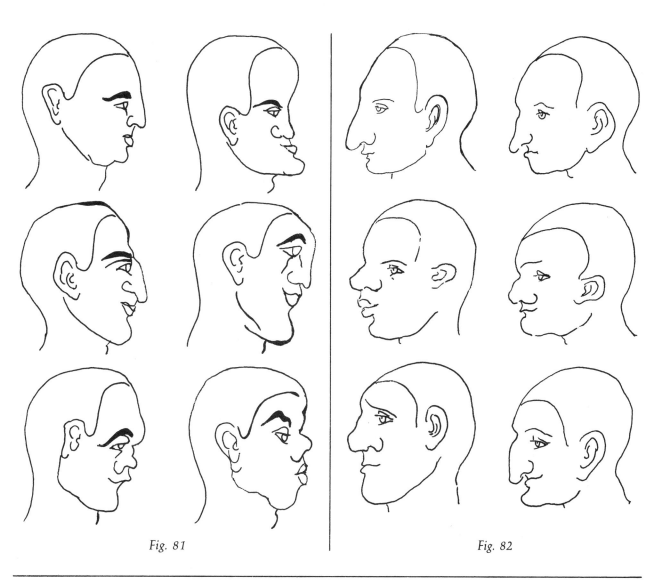

Fig. 81

Fig. 82

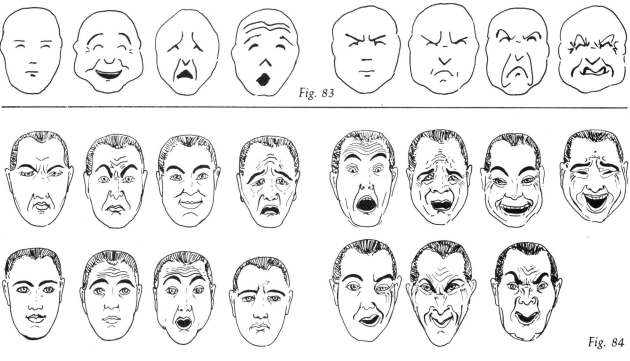

Fig. 83

Fig. 84

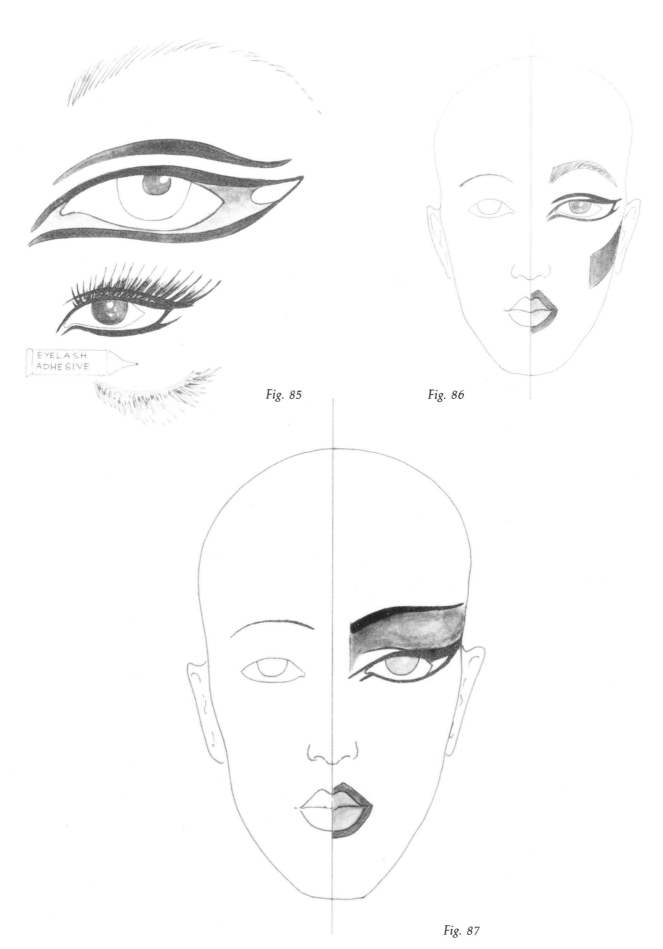

EYELASH
ADHESIVE

Fig. 85

Fig. 86

Fig. 87

Theatrical Lights

MAKE-UP COLORS	Blue	Yellow	Pink	Green	Purple	Red	Azure	Orange
Blue	Dark blue	Very dark green	Intense blue	Very dark green	Blue	Very dark blue	Light blue	Very dark blue
Yellow	Milk and coffee	White	Intense yellow	Dark yellow	Salmon	White	Light yellow	White
Red	Very dark blue	Bright red	Orange	Almost black	Bright red	Flesh color	Dark red	Highlights
Green	Very dark grey	Light green	Dull ambered-green	Light brown	Grey-blue	Dark brown	Green-light brown	Grey-green
Purple	Very high lighted, approaching azure	Ambered-grey	Intense purple	Grey	Intense azure	Blue	Purple-blue	Grey-purple
Orange	Dark grey-blue	Pale orange	Highlights	Brown	Electric rosy-orange	Yellowish ivory	Warm brown	Pastel orange
Pink	Ice white	Pastel rosy-orange	Intense pink	Ash beige	Peachy pink	Very pale pink	Lilac	Warm beige
Azure	White	Bright green	Intense azure	Ash pale azure	Electric azure	Purple	Highlights	Grey

Period Hairstyles and Make-Up

In this chapter, we'll take a very quick look at the major hairstyles and make-up from early Egypt to the present day. This section is certainly not intended to be a full-fledged study of hair or hairstyles. Many masterful texts are available on the subject of hair, but I hope this will be useful as a quick-reference tool for those occasions when you just don't have time to do countless hours of research.

Egyptians

The classic Egyptian features (Fig. 88) are regular, with complexions ranging from olive to light brown. Noses are broad and lips full, usually with a regular outline.

Shaved heads were common among ancient Egyptians, and children often wore a braid that came down over the ear on the shaved nape of the neck.

Fig. 88

Dignitaries and officials wore wigs: The ones the dignitaries wore weren't too elaborate, but those of the officials were really quite grand, with special accessories on the forehead. They often reached down to the shoulders and were sometimes braided in the back.

Colored cloth headpieces and gowns were worn by the pharaohs—red for kings of Low Egypt, white for High Egypt)—and soldiers wore two-colored plumes, one above each ear, in their wigs. The most commonly used colors were greens, blacks, reds, and whites (always from natural dyes), and wigs were dyed blue, red, and green.

Eyes were heavily lined with black (Fig. 89), and black was also used to darken lashes and brows. Eyelids generally matched wig color. Lips and cheeks were colored red.

Fig. 89

The body was often heavily oiled and looked shiny. Women dressed loose hair or braided it into in little braids. Some of them wore black squared-off wigs decorated at the top with flowers. Tiaras and crowns were worn only by the queen. Later on, when the Romans took over, the Egyptians adapted their fashions, which we'll see further on.

Arabs and Bedouins

Through the centuries Arabs (Fig. 90) have covered their heads with square cloths which protect them from the sun. Young women often wore red, old women, black.

The way Bedouins (Fig. 90) dressed their hair depended on the tribe they belonged to: some braided it, some left it loose. Some of them put small coral bells in their very thick curls. Men often wore moustaches, occasionally with a very long beard.

Fig. 90

Assyrians and Persians

Assyrians and Persians (Fig. 91) often parted their hair in the middle. Beards were left to grow naturally or were elaborately crimped and often dyed with henna in tones ranging from rust to orange.

Hair was straight, always loose on the shoulders, and ears were left uncovered.

Assyrians often wore crowns, whereas the Persians favored tiaras and sometimes wigs.

Mouth and cheeks were made up in amber shades. Eyes were lined with kohl, while black was used for underlining brows (men's especially), until they almost met in the middle.

The eye outline was often very heavy—though not as heavy as that of the Egyptians.

49

Fig. 91

Jews

Jews (Fig. 92) are usually portrayed with long hair, often covered by headgear of some kind. Young men especially wore long and flowing hair, whereas adults were more likely to wear it short along with a beard, since it was the custom not to cut the hair around the temples. Hair was dressed in this way through the centuries even into the twentieth century.

Many women wore their hair gathered in a thick, silk and gold net. They rarely used much make-up, if any.

Greeks

In Greece, both men and women paid close attention not only to hairstyles (Fig. 93) but to beautifying the face and body. In Homer's time, hair was worn loose and

Fig. 92

flowing. Gods and goddesses were depicted with such hairstyles, along with elaborate decorations—braids, curls, and ribbons. Men wore well-groomed beards and moustaches.

Pomades and oils were used to perfume and brighten the body, and men wore them as well as women. Cheeks and lips were colored red on olive complexions. Prior to the fifth century, women wore very elaborate hairstyles embellished with golden trinkets, ribbons, and sometimes precious jewelry. In that period men (generally blond), often dyed their hair red, gold, or blue.

One famous hairstyle was often worn in the theatre by actors playing satyrs and fauns. It was called "Keras," and it was done by pulling the hair completely towards the temples, into the shape of a couple of horns.

Actors also wore "oneos," triangular-shaped wigs of different sizes, depending on the importance of the actor: The more important players wore very large ones.

Around 460 B.C., hair was gathered on the temples and curled upwards to the top of the head and secured with colored pins and metallic decorations. Then came some radical changes. Men's hair was cut short and worn less elaborately—though it was always kept neat. Even old people cut their hair short so that it fell just to about the nape of the neck.

After the fifth century B.C., drastic changes took place in women's hairstyles, too, with the emphasis on simplicity. Hair was parted in the middle, fell softly along the sides of the face, and was coiled at the back with braided ribbons.

The same customs were followed by Athenians, with the slight difference that they let soft curls fall on their foreheads, framing the face down to the ears, which remained uncovered. On the temples they wore a large bottle curl.

Another hairstyle, equally simple, consisted of gathering the hair on the top of the head, and knotting it with ribbons, leaving the forehead bare. Among the youngest women, even simpler hairstyles were popular. They wore their hair loose in soft curls or gathered at the back and braided with golden or colored ribbons.

Around the year 350 B.C., beards disappeared and shaven faces were preferred, especially among soldiers. Hair was worn curled or twisted around wires to keep it tight and neat. In Athens, men used to curl their hair on their foreheads, while others separated their curls neatly into rows. Sometimes a few locks of curls were permitted to fall from the top of the head to the nape of the neck.

Romans

In the earliest days, the Roman men wore their hair long and were usually bearded. Later, towards the fifth century B.C., new fashions arrived from Sicily, among them, the customs of shaving beards and mous-

Fig. 93

taches and wearing very short hair (Fig. 94). Only philosophers and older men continued to wear their hair and beards in the earlier style.

Cosmetics were very popular with women (and with some men). Faces were made very pale with white powders, and lips and cheeks were rouged. It was in the fifth century B.C. that the first wigs appeared. Short hair became popular among the aristocracy, but poor people didn't cut their hair until the middle of the first century B.C.

During Caesar's reign, baldness was deemed almost shameful. When Caesar himself went bald, he appeared in public with a wreath of laurel and berries.

Fig. 94

Later—during the period of the Antonines (around the second century A.D.)—well-groomed, curled beards made a brief appearance and in a short time became a popular fashion, together with curled hair. Hair was always cut short, except among young Romans who often wore it long and thick, in elaborately curly styles. This gave men a feminine look that was much admired at the time. The first wigs, including many complicated and elaborate ones, date back to that time. Often they were worn to hide baldness.

In those days, dyeing the hair was very common. The Emperor Commodus in the second century A.D. dyed his with a golden powder greased with perfumed ointment.

Women's hairstyles were very simple at

the start, but they became more and more elaborate. In fact, at one time they parted their hair in the middle and coiled it with needles.

By the middle of the first century B.C., unmarried women combed their hair upwards towards the top of the head and coiled on the nape of the neck. Married women parted their hair in the center. It wasn't until the Empire (27 B.C.) that hairstyles became complicated. In some cases, hair was curled all around the head with many little spiral curls around the face. In other cases, hair was braided; the braids were brought together over the head until they met and then were pinned high on the back of the head.

Among the lower classes, hairstyles were simpler: parted in the middle, the hair fell softly on the sides and was gathered in the back.

By the end of the first century A.D., hairstyles had become whimsical and odd. Huge wigs were in great demand. The most popular were fan-shaped, made up of many layers of thick curls. The hair was braided with wire spirals to give the wig strength and keep it in shape.

When this craze died down, hair was worn in soft chignons, but the odd wigs of the first century had left their mark and during the next four centuries, other odd styles and enormous wigs came into vogue in such colors as red, turquoise, white, yellow, and blue!

After the wars along the northern borders of the Empire, the Romans started to tint their hair copper, probably in imitation of the Gauls, but in 680 A.D., with the Council of Constantinople, wigs and dyes were outlawed.

Men's Hairstyles—the Middle Ages to the Present

The Gauls, Germans, and Bretons wore their hair in fairly unusual styles, shaving their beards, but sporting rather large moustaches (Fig. 95a).

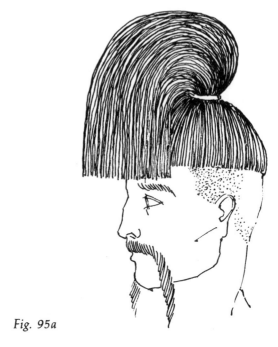

Fig. 95a

Fig. 95b

The Germans often braided their hair and coiled it on the top of the head (Fig. 95b). The Gauls bleached their hair with lime water.

In the ninth century, hair was cut short in front and left long in the back (Fig. 96a). Later on, hats and other headgear began to be worn.

It wasn't until the tenth century that hair was regularly kept longer, and at this time, Germans began to wear beards again (Fig. 96b).

The late twelfth century called for very short hair on the top of the head and long, wavy hair at the back. Men were either

Fig. 96a

Fig. 96b

VII became bald and persuaded the men of his court to shave their heads completely or at least partially. This brought about the appearance of headgear made of precious metals or soft hats that covered the head (Fig. 96d).

Fig. 96d

beardless or separated their beards into sections with thick, hooked curls that were often hardened with wax. Moustaches too were well-groomed and waxed. The most whimsical hairstyle was worn by noblemen of the thirteenth century; braided hair on the top, full hair on the forehead, and bottle curls at the sides.

During the reign of Charles VII in the mid-fifteen century, the "Edward's Son" style became fashionable. It featured short hair on the forehead and long hair in the back (Fig. 96c). As time went on, Charles

Fig. 96c

In many other countries, beards remained in fashion. It became popular to wear the hair flat over the top of the head and full all around it through the reign of Louis XI in the late fifteenth century.

Then, with Charles VIII, long hair came back, cut squarely in front, with fringe on the forehead and wavy at the ends. (Fig. 96e).

In the sixteenth century, sudden changes took place in hairstyles. In 1520, men had been beardless and wore their hair cut high at the crown (Fig. 97). In 1521, when Francis I received a headwound, hair returned to the completely shaven style. At that time pointed beards were also in fashion. Calvinists wore a hairstyle that originated during the reign of Charles IX (1560–1574), which consisted of shaving the hair in the back and replacing it with a hairpiece.

Fig. 96e

After that, Henry IV of France (1589–1610) created a hair sensation when he combed his hair upwards to cover some cotton padding in an apple or pear shape. The beard became thicker, but remained pointed (Fig. 97). During this period, Germans and Scandinavians wore their hair short, with thick beards.

The *"à l'enfant"* style, devised by Louis XIII, followed in the seventeenth century, with thick curled hair and sparse moustache—well groomed and waxed, with the ends turned outward like hooks. Beards

Fig. 97

56

were always pointed and extremely neat (Fig. 98a). Toupees were still in style.

At the end of the reign of Louis XIII in 1643, hair continued to be worn long and curled down to the shoulders. Full-bottomed wigs—made of artificial hair built up over the natural hair—appeared. During the same period bald people often wore a black cap on which long hair was attached (Fig. 98b). Also enormously popular: a wig with full bottle curls (Fig. 99).

Fig. 98a

Fig. 98b

Fig. 99

After 1640, moustaches and beards disappeared, except among old men, priests, and doctors. Under Louis (1643–1715) (Fig. 100), wigs became long and elaborate, in colors ranging from black to maroon to white, from wavy to tightly curled. First there was a great preference for blond wigs, and then, later, for black ones. It was about this time that it became fashionable to add an artificial beauty spot to the chin. Moustaches were kept in a hooked shape with wax, while the rest of the face was carefully shaven. During the reign of Louis XV, when France set the laws of fashion, wigs became less popular. Hair was left to grow, and hairstyles were divided into three sections: forehead, braid, and toupee (Fig. 101).

Hairstylists were much sought after. They invented the "bags," an imitation of a Prussian fashion. The bags consisted of little black silk bags which held the back hair on the nape of the neck, while side hair was cut away from the face, leaving it clear with ears exposed.

Around 1740, nobles powdered their hair. The middle class followed suit, but they used corn flour colored in grey, pink, light blue, and yellow. The working class gathered their hair in the back and let it grow to shoulder length.

At that time, mostly in Germany, moustaches were fashionable, especially among military men. After 1750, and during the next half century, the use of "bags" remained in style, but the shape of hair around the face changed. The hair at the sides of the face was curled and decorated with ribbons (Fig. 102).

After this, hair was left to grow; it began to cover the sides of the face, and run down

Fig. 100

Fig. 101

Fig. 102

the back over the shoulders. At this point, the Greek toupee came into style—a huge, pointed headpiece measuring from four to five inches at each side.

Braids became less popular among the nobility and a very simple hairstyle appeared. It was called "Catogan" and it consisted of knotting the back hair. At this time clergymen wore their hair long and curled. With the French Revolution and the Abbot Siéyès, many people wore their hair very simply, short and combed forward. One popular hairstyle of the day was called

Fig. 103a

"dog and duck"; the sides were either curled or straight and worn long over the shoulders. Some men wore their hair in entirely unique styles that were their own personal choices (Brissot and Marat, for example, Fig. 103a).

Fig. 103b

Fig. 104

After the Reign of Terror (1794), it became fashionable to do hair in the "victim" style—very short at the back, long in the front, partly covering the eyes, like convicts who were condemned to death. For the most elegant, fashion required long hair in the back as well (Fig. 103b).

Fig. 105

Fig. 106

parte hairstyles were still worn. Side hair was kept in shape with wax, combed forward, and sometimes combined with a toupee. This style continued—mostly among the aristocracy—until 1848 (Fig. 105).

In 1860, short beards and moustaches were in vogue. Romantics also wore their hair short, parted at the middle or at the side (Fig. 106). By the end of the 1800s, beards disappeared almost completely and smooth, well-groomed, end-curled moustaches took their place.

Short hair, parted and combed upward or to the side (Fig. 107), remained popular for a long time.

Towards 1918, a medium-short cut at the front and the almost total lack of hair at the nape of the neck became the fashionable style (Fig. 108).

Short hair, more or less wavy, kept in shape with wax or brilliantine, was the predominant style without any particular changes until the arrival of Elvis Presley with his famous pompadour in the 1950s, meticulously styled with many coats of brilliantine and then later, done in a more natural way (Fig. 109 on page 64).

In 1964, with the advent of the Beatles, a new style caught on among young people. Longer hair became the fashion in many countries, and it was done in many different styles (Fig. 110a). In fact, from 1964 to 1970, hair length followed an irregular course, but as far as style was concerned, it certainly improved. Long hair—with fringes, slightly curled or frizzed, with flowing locks combed back—remained in fashion until 1978, when short cuts began to reappear recalling the styles of the 1920s (Fig. 110b).

In the 1980s, among young people, long, styled hair in front, often artificially curled with back hair shaven on the nape of the neck, became de rigueur. In America, brilliantined hair (Elvis's style) was still popular (Fig. 111). Middle-aged men, these days, generally wear a classic short cut without any special features.

Later, with the Directory (1795–1799), fashion returned to some of its previous styles: Hair was curled, dyed blond, and kept in place with perfumed oils.

With Napoleon Bonaparte, short hair became fashionable again, due, of course, to the fact that Napoleon himself wore a short cut (Fig. 104). It remained popular, too, for a long time and spread throughout Europe, although during the Restoration, powdered, full-bottomed wigs reappeared.

Moustaches were extremely important in fashion at that time. They were often curled to make them appear more showy. With Louis Philippe (the first half of the nineteenth century), some short-length Bona-

Fig. 107

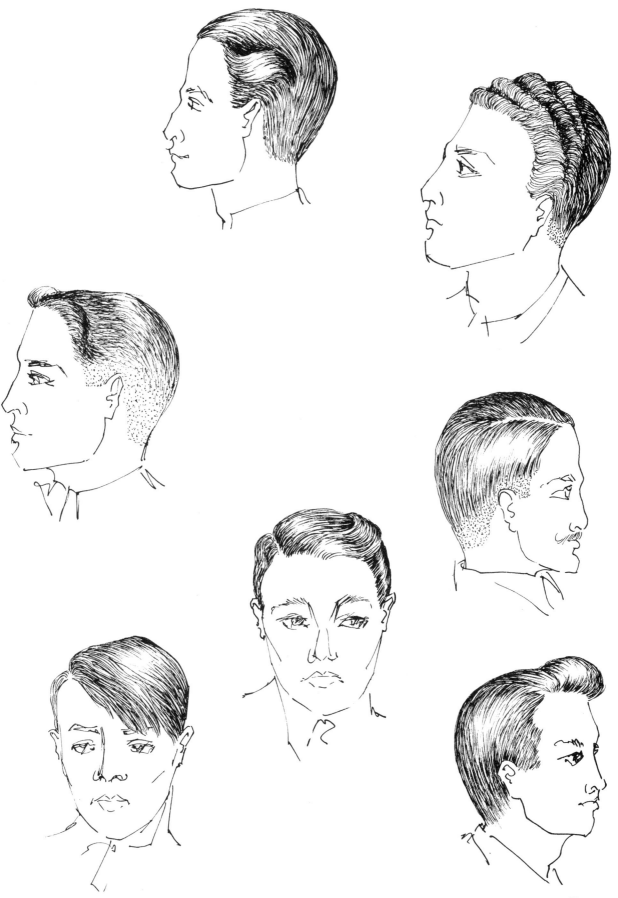

Fig. 108

Fig. 109

Fig. 110a

Fig. 110b

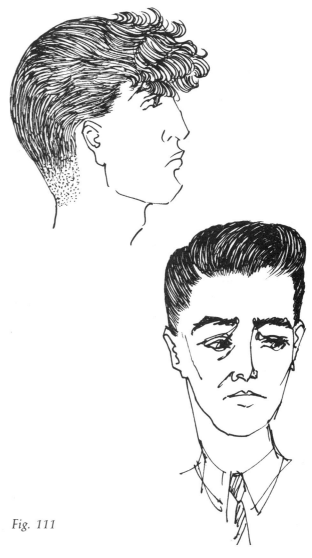

Fig. 111

Women's Hairstyles—Middle Ages to the Present

Light, tinted locks, hanging loosely on the shoulders, this was the style of Gaulish women. Hair was often parted in the middle and gathered in braids on the sides of the head (Fig. 112). Sometimes women wore headgear. Later on, hair was decorated with jewels, perfumed, or waved at the temples and held in place with a golden barrette.

From the end of the tenth century, almost every woman wore her hair relatively straight under transparent veils, rarely showing it off. Many of the more wealthy wore velour headgear studded with jewels and light veils (Fig. 113).

During the thirteenth century, women often gathered their hair in embroidered snoods, or wore bonnets held on by a strip of velvet that ran under the chin and framed the face.

In the early fourteenth century, hair was braided on the forehead with some locks around the cheekbones. It was popular to dye the hair blond or black (dyeing it red was considered utterly wicked, and few did

Fig. 112

Fig. 113

it). To avoid showing their hair, women of the fifteenth century used to wear headgear that revealed—at the temples—only a coiled braid and perhaps a lock of hair at the forehead. Their remaining hair was

gathered high in the back. In the late fifteenth century, it became fashionable to let the forehead show. Hair was then braided and coiled at the sides of the head, in a horn-shaped arrangement. This particular hairstyle was actually nicknamed "horns." Sometimes the horns were extremely large, and on some occasions they were covered with veils or with light embroidered material.

Tall, peaked headgear became fashionable from 1370 to 1470. It hid the hair completely, except for a carefully arranged lock of hair on the forehead. At court, women preferred to conceal their hair with crowns, jewels, and gold trinkets.

Immediately afterward, hair was again worn flat on the head and covered with beribboned bonnets. Some women began to wear their hair long in the back, which was then arranged, completely curled in the front and finally down the back again. In any case, the hair was worn long (Fig. 114).

In the sixteenth century, three types of hairstyles came into fashion. The first was known as the "Tuscan coiffure." The hair was gathered at the back and held with a jewel-studded ribbon, which wound around the head over the forehead. A decorated cap was worn on the top of the head.

In the second style, the "Spanish coiffure," a decorated velour scarf was draped over the head and held in place by a plume at the side (take a look at any of Mary Stuart portraits for examples of this).

For the "French coiffure," a small cap was held on the head by pearls and veils.

With Charles IX (until around 1630), women began to powder their hair and built it high up in curls over very thin, round wire frames. Sometimes hair was also curled (Fig. 115). The fashion of wearing wigs dates back to that period (for men as well as women). During summer months, light bonnets—that reached from the forehead to the nape of the neck—replaced the wigs.

Around 1630, wigs were on the way out. Hair was combed flat on the head, coiled in

Fig. 114

the back, curled on the forehead and sides and decorated with plumes on the top (Fig. 116).

At the end of that century, women began to curl their hair and hide their faces with masks, except when they visited or received important personages.

A real passion started in the late seventeenth century for beauty marks—almost everyone wore them and their placement was actually significant: A beauty mark close to the eye implied that a lady was passionate. A beauty mark beside the

Fig. 115

Fig. 116

mouth suggested that she was sensuous, and one on the cheek meant that she was flirtatious, and there were more.

Face make-up was widely used, and red was the chosen color.

Around 1670, hair in front was separated into tidy sections of flat curls reaching down to the ears, and back hair was coiled (Fig. 117). One hairstyle, called the "Fontange" style because Mlle de Fontanges started it, was particularly popular from 1680 until 1692. Actually, it was not so much one hairstyle as a number of variations on the theme of gathered and knotted hair. The hair might be combed with curls at the temples (called "favorites") and coiled at the back, or it might be twisted around some kind of cap. It might be curled and puffed and held by ribbons, falling over the ears and forehead, or with curls knotted on the top and a couple of bottle curls falling down the sides (Fig. 118).

Fig. 117

The hairstyle worn by another woman, Madame de Maintenon, took over from this fashion and imposed a more serious formal style, with straight hair in front, gathered in little bonnets (Figs. 119–20).

In 1730, hairstyles became exaggeratedly high. During the period from 1765 to 1770, practically every fashionable woman adopted Grecian hairstyles. After this, wig fashions became all the rage with some wigs reaching as high as fifty-one inches tall! The wigs were decorated with everything from jewels, flowers, and plumes to small ceramic statues and chains! In the time of Marie Antoinette, fantastic wigs—such as the one with the sailing ship (Fig. 121)—were a sensation throughout Europe.

Elaborate hairstyles disappeared around

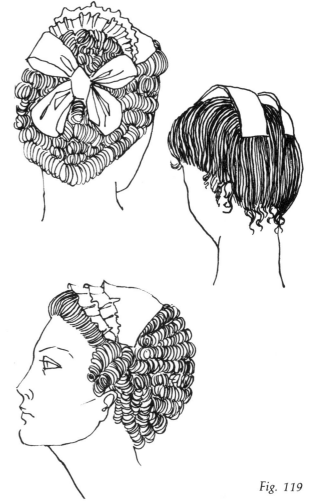

Fig. 119

Fig. 118

1780 because of the Queen's baldness. She began combing her hair flat with a back coil that ended in a bottle curl. Naturally, that subdued style became the fashion. Huge hats were often worn with this hairstyle, which, with the French Revolution, assumed various shapes. Under the hat, hair was often left soft and flowing and curling over forehead, cheekbones, neck, and shoulders (Fig. 122 on page 74).

During the Directory (1795–1799), wigs came back into style—blond ones for the morning and black ones for the night.

With the beginning of the nineteenth century in France, it was fashionable to wear a coil at the side of the face, leaving one lock of hair free to fall delicately along the neck.

From the time of Napoleon to the Empire (1804–1815), French women were cutting their hair shorter, curling and dressing it

Fig. 120

Fig. 121

73

Fig. 122

high, often with an embroidered ribbon (Fig. 123).

During the Restoration (1824–1850), there was great diversity. Some women separated their hair into two sections, combing it smoothly on the top of the head and curled immediately under the ears. Some wore large bottle curls at the sides or soft puffs at the temples.

In 1852, simplicity became more popular: hair was flat, gathered in a ribbon, and loose around the neck. This phase lasted until around 1860, when another style took over, and for the next five years hair was dressed high, dyed blond and reddish, and when it wasn't showy enough, worn with very large hats (Fig. 124).

During the years after 1870, hairpieces came into vogue, often worn with fringes and gathered in a simple way. Sometimes silk flowers were incorporated into the hairstyle on the nape of the neck, while soft curls framed the face, falling over the forehead and temples (Fig. 125 on page 77).

Around 1900, hair was wavy, generally swept up, leaving the neck exposed, and combed in neat curls on the forehead. Combs made of precious or semi-precious materials and plumes were always in fashion (Fig. 126). The most popular style around 1902 featured hair swept up and fastened at the nape of the neck (Fig. 127).

From 1902 to 1910, styles didn't change much. Some women combed their hair low

Fig. 123

Fig. 124

Fig. 125

Fig. 126

Fig. 127

Fig. 128

Fig. 129a

on the forehead, dividing it into two sections and decorating it with rhinestone necklaces. Others wore soft braids (sometimes false ones) around the back of the head and the top of the head to make the hairstyle higher (Fig. 128). False braids were kept in place by pretty combs or rhinestone beads and tiaras.

Around 1911, large hats, often adorned with plumes on upper *and* lower brims, were popular again. Hair was short and precisely waved (Fig. 129a). Women who kept it long often coiled their hair on top of their heads or at the nape of the neck (Fig. 129b).

After 1915—in 1917, to be exact—wavy, upswept styles were popular with curls covering forehead and temples, reaching along the sides of the cheeks. In 1921, back hair was dressed very high, and the forehead was always covered with curls (Fig. 130 on page 81).

In 1922, in came the "page boy" style: very short hair with straight bangs, or combed completely back, leaving a lock—more or less thick—reaching from the temples, down the cheeks (Fig. 131).

From 1930 to 1938, the same short cut became more elaborate: hair was parted at the side, curled, and waved. Around 1938, hairstyles became more subdued in height and length. Often hair was swept up with just a few curls falling down in the back, with a side or front lock or curl to complete the style (Fig. 132 on page 82).

By 1945, bottle curls and upswept hairdos were in, sometimes with braids encircling the head. Braids were also used on top of the head, with the rest of the hair falling loosely in waves to the shoulders. Hairpins were used frequently. Some women parted their short hairstyles in the middle all the way from the forehead to the nape of the neck, forming curly horns at the sides, while a lock of hair covered the forehead (Fig. 133 on page 82).

About 1950 and until 1960, short cuts and hair curled in many different ways (Fig.

Fig. 129b

Fig. 130

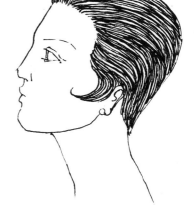

Fig. 131

Fig. 132 | *Fig. 133*

Fig. 134

Fig. 135

Fig. 136

134) became fashionable again. While from 1962 to 1970 hairdos changed a great deal few styles left their mark except for the "Sassoon" (1965) and the "Afro" (1969). During those years hair was worn in many different ways: gathered high, with bangs, side curls, bottle curls, and fancy upsweeps that sometimes incorporated ribbons. The only characteristic feature of that time was a technical innovation: "teasing" (Fig. 135).

Around 1975, shorter cuts appeared (Fig. 136), but basically, every woman seemed determined to do her own thing, as far as hairstyles were concerned. You'd see many women with quite short hair and others with lots of long hair. Prior to this time most women seemed to prefer short, neat haircuts, except for a brief return to the forties' look in around 1979, and the braids that became so popular around 1980. Today it is considered important to comb and dress short hair, with styled forelocks and back length perfectly scaled down to the nape of the neck.

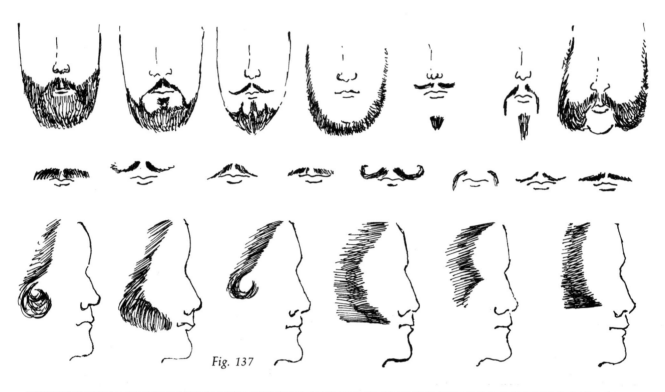

Fig. 137

Fig. 138

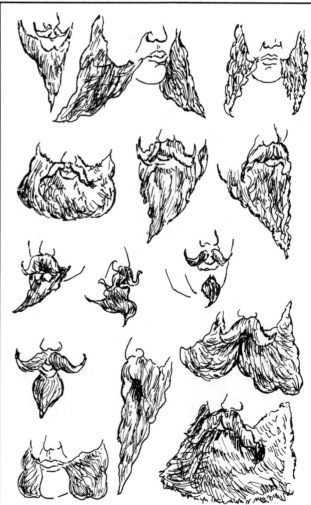

Fig. 139

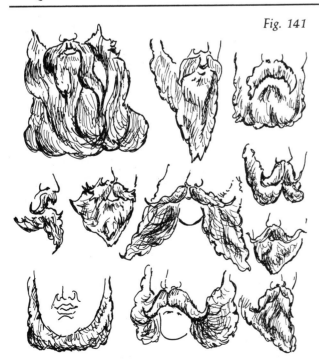

Fig. 140

Fig. 141

Beards and Moustaches Throughout the Centuries

Throughout the centuries, beards and moustaches have gone through an immense variety of styles (Figs. 137–141).

In the time of the Egyptians, they were not commonly used. Only Pharaohs wore beards—which were squared, wider at the bottom where they were finally curled.

Hebrews, Assyrians, and Moabites had thick beards, because in those days shaving was considered unlucky. Assyrians kings wore their beards carefully braided into tufts. Oriental kings decorated them with golden threads. The ancient Greeks adorned their faces with pointed, short, and precise beards that left the upper lip clear.

The Spartans considered the beard so prestigious that when they inflicted a heavy penalty, part of the beard was shaved off. They usually sported untrimmed beards, while the Athenians gave their beards particular care and attention. No one style of beard was worn by all the Greeks—and beards were not worn universally. Often a famous artist or character could be found bearded one time and unbearded another, depending upon the artist. At the time of Alexander the Great, beards were worn when in mourning, and they were considered a bad omen. The only ones who continued to wear them were the philosophers—except for Aristotle, whose face was completely shaven.

With the Romans, beards and moustaches returned until about 300 B.C. After that, even the Romans began to shave completely. This was done generally at around age 40; up until that time the beard was kept short and neat, leaving the upper lip uncovered. But after that age, not shaving was thought of as bringing imminent bad luck.

Having a shaven face remained fashionable for all of Caesar's kingdom up until the time of the Emperor Trajan (98–117 A.D.). Occasionally, beards came back into vogue: With the Emperor Constantine, faces were completely shaved; with Julian, beards were worn once again; then for almost two centuries they disappeared completely.

Orientals, Mohammedans, and Byzantine kings wore very long and differently shaped beards, while the Gauls wore them pointed. Generally, nobles wore only moustaches, and if they wore beards at all they wore the soft-pointed "stiletto" type. The Gauls used to dye all their hair red.

Thick, quite long moustaches and carefully shaven beards were characteristic of German tribes. Later on, beards were worn shorter and braided with golden threads.

In the sixth century, among the French, beards and moustaches disappeared, except for the small, pointed "stiletto" type, but they returned in the seventh century, became highly fashionable, and then disappeared again immediately after Charlemagne (early ninth century), who preferred long thick moustaches that reached down to the shoulders.

After innumerable changes, long beards returned in the tenth century—to stay for hundreds of years. During the twelfth century, when the Church condemned the practice of wearing beards as sin and damnation, penitents were forced to shave their hair, beards, and moustaches, but other men continued to wear quite long ones. In the thirteenth century, beards were braided with circular gold wires to keep them curled.

In 1340, a Spanish fashion from the Mediterranean—long moustaches and pointed beards—arrived in France. The only men who continued to shave their faces were clergymen. At the same time in Spain, artificial beards were creating a sensation.

At the beginning of the 1500s, completely shaved faces returned. Following Clement VII in the 1530s, there was a revival of beards and moustaches that included even the clergy—including pontiffs and prelates—until the reign of Louis XIV.

Henry II made the beard almost a cult.

During this period many different-shaped beards were worn: squared, pointed, fan-shaped, swallow-tailed, round, and others, too.

In the time of Henry IV, until 1628, the beard was pointed, in imitation of the King's chosen style.

It was Louis XIII in the mid 1600s who launched the fashion of the "royale"-style beard. He ordered all his soldiers to wear light, thin moustaches; beards were merely a thin tuft of hair on the chin. That style lasted until the eighteenth century. Sometimes the moustaches were so thin they were practically invisible, and some of the beards were made up of as few as fifty hairs!

By the start of the French Revolution, the Hussars discovered and adopted the style of moustache that was worn by soldiers only. That style continued during the first Empire (1804–1815). By the end of the Restoration in the mid 1800s, beards were left to grow again, and they became particularly popular in artistic, literary, and political circles. Austrian officers, at least, didn't limit themselves to wearing simple moustaches. They went much further with beards during the reigns of Nicolas I and Francis Joseph I, exemplified in the styles made popular by Austrian imperialists and the Russian bureaucracy.

With the arrival of the Second Empire in 1852, the Imperial-style beard became fashionable—a little pointed beard that one wore sometimes in conjunction with well trimmed moustaches until 1860—particularly in Latin countries. The standard-bearer of this style was Victor Emmanuel II of Italy (1849–1878), but the fashion evolved out of a style of Napoleon III.

No great changes took place after that until 1930. Before 1945, during the time of Adolf Hitler, there was a brief appearance of small moustaches, but beards were still uncommon. It wasn't until 1962, particularly in France, that beards and moustaches came back into vogue, though in a limited way.

After 1968, moustaches and beards began to be seen again. From 1970 to 1975, well-groomed beards and moustaches were very much in style. Nowadays, in almost every industrialized country, beards and moustaches are seen regularly, but the choice of whether or not to wear them and what type to wear depends more on personal choice than on fashion.

Make-up for the Nationalities

During the last decade—perhaps for even longer than that—television, the press, our rapid means of communication, and the enormous popularity of tourism have brought about a great deal of knowledge and contact among the different peoples of the world. In our study of make-up, we have to look first at the different types of skin that are characteristic of the different countries, but, of course, all characters cannot be stereotyped racially! Any advice on how—and with which shade—make-up is to be done must be taken only as a rough guideline. Even among the members of a particular race there is an immense amount of variation: one's complexion could be of a deep brown tone, for example, or have a yellowish or olive or reddish-brown cast.

In the following pages, we'll take a look at some of the different races, show a few ways to analyze them, determine the skin color to use, and look at the different make-ups required.

Europeans

The European people are basically Caucasoid, and make-up can generally be the type used for Caucasoids—with the following variations:

Mediterraneans (such as the Spanish, Portuguese, the French from the south of France, the Italians, and some Irish and Welsh)—Shades go from amber to olive-beige: Use darker tones for islanders who are exposed to sunlight for many months of the year.

Central Europeans (Austrians, the Swiss, the French from central France, the Czechoslovaks, those from the Balkans and the Soviet Union)—Use a medium shade—with a bit more red in it for the Russians.

North Europeans (Dutch, Belgians, English, Scandinavians)—Use light tones.

North Americans

Most North Americans have the same characteristics as the Europeans as far as skin tone and hair color goes.

The first inhabitants of North America—the Indians—require make-up with tones that range from honey color to reddish and yellowish brown. The hair is jet black, and they have very little facial or body hair.

Face decorations will vary from tribe to tribe, so it's advisable to consult a good textbook that discusses the geography, habits, and customs of the Indian tribe you're interested in. But there are a few facts that any good make-up artist should know:

Many Indians let their hair grow naturally, braiding it in long plaits that ran down past the shoulders to the chest.

They wore various hairstyles for different occasions. The women would often part their hair in the middle and braid it at the sides. Others wore colored headbands or bright bands around the end of the braids. Women never wore feathers. For men, however, feather headdresses meant honor and power.

Some men parted their hair in the middle and braided it, as women did. Others decorated it at the ends, parting it at the side. Still others burned their hair off or shaved it, leaving only a large central area of hair starting high on the forehead and reaching down to the nape of the neck. Some of the shaven styles left only one long lock at the top of the head (in northeastern areas). Some Indians tinted their hair white, dark blue, purple, red, or green.

COUNTRY	SKIN COLOR	HAIR
India Bengal { northeast Bihar Gujarat { west Rajasthan	pale brown-olive	straight black
Kashmir (north) Madras (south)	light brown greyish brown	straight black wavy and dark
Ceylon	dark brown	wavy, long, and black
Burma	yellowish brown	wavy and black, with sparse hair on face and body

COUNTRY	SKIN COLOR	HAIR
Malay Peninsula	chocolate brown	short, shaggy black hair, with sparse hair on face and body
Malaysia	copperish brown	shaggy and black
Bali **Borneo** **Celebes** **Java** **Philippines** **Sumatra**	light brown to yellowish	very dark and wavy, with sparse hair on face and body

Young women dressed their hair with brooches pinned high at the sides of the forehead. While in mourning, they wore their hair in a big braid that fell down to the shoulders. Almost every Indian of North America wore body dye and tattoos of one kind or another. The colors used for the decorations sometimes had a significance—war paint, for example. Red and black were the most often used colors originally, and then, with the arrival of the Europeans, blue, green, white, and yellow dyes were imported and used as well.

To get the effect of the eyebrows slanting

up towards the temples—typical of the Mongoloid race—shape the ends accordingly (see page 28 for more about how to do it), which will be good enough for background takes, though for close-ups you'll have to shave the eyebrows off or cover them. Remember, when making lashes and eyebrows, that Indian people have very dark hair. When hair is not sufficiently long, get a wig. For bald heads, use a latex cap (see instructions on page 94).

Eskimos require a yellower base make-up than the one used for Indians. To get good results, mix the reddish color used for Indians with the yellow one used for oriental make-up.

For Canadians, use the same base recommended for Northern Europeans.

Central and South Americans

The Incas, the Yucatan Mayas, and the Jivaro—South American Indians, all—should be made up in the same way as the North American Indians, except for hairstyles.

For Mexicans, use the same shades—with lighter tones such as olive or yellowish brown—for women. Eyes and hair should be very dark. Men of Spanish descent are more hairy than Mexicans or Indians.

Southwestern Asians

Asians are made up of a wide range of races and nationalities, which includes Russians, Central Europeans, Egyptians, Arabs, the Portuguese and the Spanish. Most of them are of Mediterranean descent.

For an Asian look, use make-up with beige and yellowish tones, and keep in mind that these peoples have little facial or body hair, which is very dark and frizzy.

Persians and Iranians—who often are descended from Mongoloids, Mediterranean, or Arab-Armenian forebears—should be made up with shades ranging from light brown to biscuit color.

South Asians

People from India have features that are derived from many different races, and their skin tones may vary considerably as well. On page 90, you'll see a chart that lists the most important areas of South Asia and the foundation shades you'll want to use to make up the characters. Remember that beards and moustaches are worn all over India, and that apart from skin color, the Indian race is very like the European one.

It's also useful to know that you'll find less yellowish color in the skin of Asian inhabitants the further they live away from China.

Far Easterners

Two races can be identified in the Far East: One is tall, with fine features, black hair, and almond-shaped eyes, but not of the Mongoloid type. The other is short and stocky, with heavy bones, and jet-black hair. The eyes have the classic Mongoloid fold, and the skin is slightly darker than that of the first group.

Both need to be made up with a beige shade, more or less verging on yellow.

Facial hair is usually nonexistent, and both men and women tend to age prematurely.

A noticeable detail of the eyebrow is easily recognized: hairs do not grow at the end part creating the "wing" cut.

For the Japanese race called Ainu, use a warm beige skin tone, with bushy black hair and beard. They come from an ancient Caucasoid/Mongoloid group, and are different for many reasons from the usual Japanese race.

Southern and Central Asians

People from this area, which also includes people from Tibet, Mongolia, and part of Siberia, have little hair on their face or bodies. The complexion tone ranges from very light brown to hazel-yellowish brown.

Oceanians

Races of many different skin colors can be found in Australia, Melanesia, Polynesia, New Guinea, Tasmania, and Micronesia, which are included under the heading of Oceania—the territory that reaches from Australia to the Isle of Papua New Guinea, and from New Zealand to Hawaii. In Australia, of course, the great majority of the population are Caucasoid, and Northern European in skin tone. The Aborigines, however, have a chocolate-brown skin tone, very curly black hair, and a remarkable growth of beard (this group is actually a Caucasoid and Negroid combination).

Generally, the inhabitants of Melanesia have dark curly hair, with little of it on face or body. Polynesians and Hawaiians have very dark hair, which is straight or just slightly wavy. All of the island people of Oceania have a dark olive to medium-brown skin color.

The Papuans and the Melanesians belong to an Aboriginal-Australian race that lived in Tasmania until about the end of the nineteenth century and then gave way to the English immigrants. They had the same features and hair color of the Australian Aborigines.

Micronesia includes the Mariannas, the Marshall Islands, the Carolinas, and Gilbert Island, and it is populated by people of the Caucasoid-Negroid race, with skin tones verging on medium yellowish brown. They generally have frizzy black hair.

Africans

The Africans living in the territories of the upper Nile, the northernmost areas and on the west coast—along with the Hottentots, Bushmen, and Pygmies—have a skin tone that ranges from light yellowish brown to very dark brown. In some of these countries, you'll also see body dyeing and tattooing. The most common colors are usually the same ones used by the American Indians to color their bodies—blue, white, yellow—but the designs and their meanings are different. Their hair is generally frizzy, black, and often knotted and curled. Many of the African tribes decorate their heads with very complicated hairstyles and headgear. Among these people you can also find Albinos, with light skin and hair that is almost white. The African races of the north and northeastern areas belong to the Caucasoid race. They have dark or reddish-brown skin. Their hair is frizzy and dark, too (often black) and curled or waved.

Arabs and Jews have skin of an amber olive color (darker for men, more or less intense olive color for women) and usually dark hair. Among the men, beards and moustaches are common.

White Africans live principally in the Republic of South Africa where settlers from Holland and Great Britain imposed European civilization. They would be similar in skin tone to the Northern Europeans, with straight black, blond, or red hair.

Changing the Appearance

Putty and Derma Wax

There are several quick and easy ways to change the appearance. One of them is adding derma wax, a puttylike material, to face and body. Used in theatre and television—very seldom in films—it is applied in areas that don't move much, because even if you use the best adhesives with it, it shifts naturally as the muscles and skin shift. For that reason it's never used when close-up shots are required.

Let's say you want to add a bump to the nose. Moisten a little brush in spirit gum and wet the area involved (Fig. 142).

Add a few tufts of cotton (Fig. 143) to create a consistency that the putty will adhere to. Then soften the putty with your fingers. When it is flexible enough, apply it to the nose (Fig. 144) and press it into shape with modelling tools and your fingers, which should be lubricated with petroleum jelly, soap, and alcohol.

Once you get the shape right, pat the lump with a red rubber sponge or a

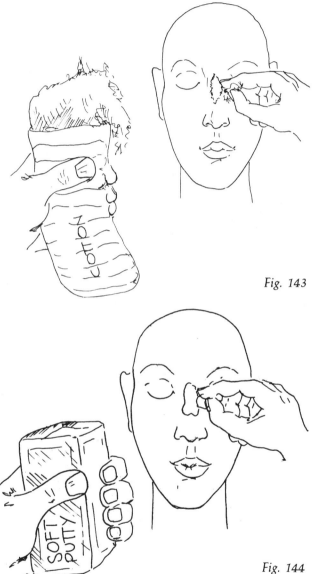

Fig. 143

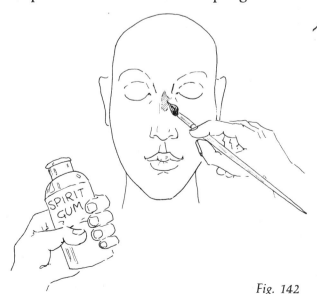

Fig. 142

Fig. 144

sponge-tipped applicator (Fig. 145), to create the look of skin pores. Next moisten a Chinese brush in a soapy solution. Dry it. Then use it to apply a layer of fixative to the entire area in which you're working, spreading it out beyond the edges of the wax (Fig. 146).

Finally, dry the wax using a hairdryer, and apply cream stick or a colored founda-

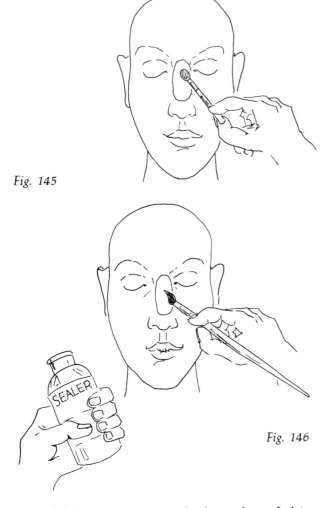

Fig. 145

Fig. 146

very thin sheet of foil (this is available through special sources). You may also find it in the inner wrapping of some candies. First check to see if the person has a sensitivity to metallic substances. Make the tooth perfectly dry before you cover it. Start by applying a thin coat of spirit gum. Wait for a few minutes and then, carefully, with tweezers, make the foil adhere to the tooth. Remove the excess foil. Smooth and flatten the surface with small dental tools until it looks real. Of course, the actor who wears this foil tooth will not be able to chew, but otherwise, it should be all right. Note: *Never* use foil on a false or coated tooth.

Some make-up artists create false teeth themselves, using dental cement. Some of them make complete casts, but to do that you need a laboratory full of tools and equipment. It is more sensible to consult a good dental technician. If you need some special effect, provide sketches of the look you want, and take the actor to the technician for the work to be done.

You may be able to get a passable, rough effect, using ready-made false teeth from a dental supply house, and applying them over the real teeth using temporary dental cement. When the performance is over, just pull off the artificial teeth and, with a hard brush and water, clean off both the real teeth and the hollow of the false ones so you can use them again.

tion. Make sure to match the color of this base to the "new" nose, which will be a lighter color.

Powder liberally and spray with a make-up fixative.

Tooth Make-up

Tooth enamels are available in several colors: black, white, tobacco, red, gold, and silver, which you can mix together to get other shades. They are used to create the illusion of decayed or missing teeth, and are easy to remove with a cotton ball moistened in alcohol.

You can also use black wax to block out teeth or get the effect of decayed teeth and gums. Experiment with it, and you'll get the results you want.

To create the look of gold or silver teeth, you may want to cover the real tooth with a

Bald Heads

It takes a great deal of patience to achieve a realistic bald look. All make-up artists today—whether working in theatre, films, or video—save time and work by using plastic and latex caps that they order from make-up suppliers or manufacturers. But even though the caps are ready to use, you still need to take great care in order to get them to look right, and it helps to have an assistant working in collaboration with you.

First of all, gather the hair in such a way

that it lies extremely flat, without leaving any ridges or protruding shapes. It's easier to do this, of course, if the actor has short hair to begin with—or is willing to cut it. But in any case, one way to gather up the hair is to soap it with glycerine soap (Fig. 147) and then dry it with a hairdryer.

Now pull a small, tight cap onto the head, which will create a base for the actual cap to be used. This small cap will be tight enough so that folds and protrusions disappear.

After that, pull on the actual plastic cap loosely (Fig. 148) and with a honey-colored pencil draw an outline on it about half an inch from the hairline.

Take the cap off and cut along the outline you just marked, using sharp scissors (Fig. 149).

Now put the cap on again. When it's smooth and in perfect position, glue down the part over the forehead, using a thin brush and spirit gum (Fig. 150).

Press and flatten the edges with a clean cloth that has no threads on it that could come off on the face.

Then, delicately but firmly, pull the cap towards the sideburns (Fig. 151) while your assistant pulls—in the same delicate way—the other side and the back of the cap.

Then glue (Fig. 152) one side at a time, pressing lightly and flattening the cap with the clean cloth. Finally, glue the area behind the ears.

Attaching the back of the cap sometimes creates problems, and for this reason many make-up artists leave the area clear—without adhesive—so the character has complete freedom of movement. You can easily do this if you plan to add a wig over the cap, or when the back of the cap will not be visible. But in other cases, you will need to glue the back down.

You might want to suggest that the actor or actress should get an extremely short haircut. High up on the neck area, even fine hairs will have to be shaven off so as to get a smooth surface on which to attach the cap. Of course, the cap should be attached at the highest point so that the actor can have as much freedom of movement as possible.

Finally, the edges of the cap can be hidden by going over it a few times with a cotton swab dipped in acetone (Fig. 153), and dotting the latex to obtain a realistic effect. It will also help to add a layer of fixative with a Chinese brush so that the edges flow more smoothly into the area to be made up and give it a less artificial look (Fig. 154).

When all these layers are dry, spread cream stick or greasepaint with a thin rubber sponge (Fig. 155). Powder abundantly to eliminate excess greasiness.

To remove the cap, loosen the edges with a cotton ball moistened in acetone. Keep in mind that if you remove the cap carefully, you'll be able to use it a second time, especially if the use is limited to television.

The make-up for a bald head consists of applying a foundation over the entire scalp. But the make-up for a plastic-cap bald head is obtained by blending the area with a bluish-grey color. Powder liberally, removing the excess powder with a soft brush.

To get the same effect, there's another method which gives excellent results if you use it for stage and video. You can even use it for films provided that you do it very carefully and use it only to simulate a few bald areas of the head—not the whole head.

Starting from the outer edges of the area you want to cover, soap up the hair horizontally, using glycerine soap mixed with just a bit of water. Soap it in horizontal bands (Figs. 156 and 157), until you have covered the entire area you want to make bald (Figs. 158 and 159).

Comb it while you flatten it as much as possible with the soap. Dry it section by section, with a hairdryer, until the treated area is all crusty and dry (Fig. 160).

Paint a layer of spirit gum over the whole area, and then apply a piece of thin, light-colored nylon pantyhose (Figs. 161 and 162). Be sure to cut the nylon strip accurately to fit the soaped area so that it's ex-

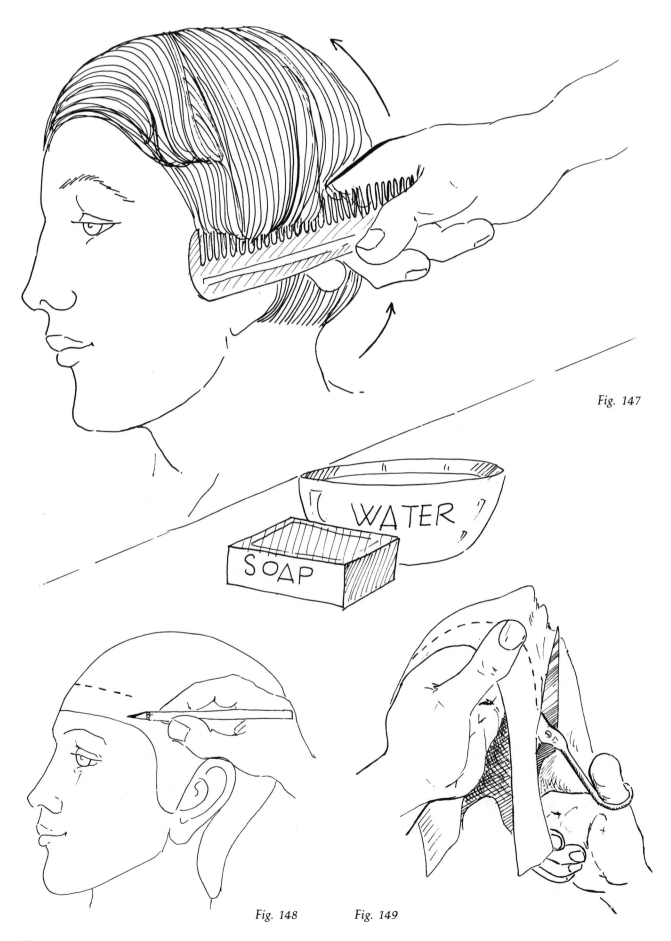

Fig. 147

WATER

SOAP

Fig. 148   Fig. 149

Fig. 150

actly the size and shape of the area you want to make bald. Pat it down with your fingers—wrapped up in another strip of nylon—to get the nylon to adhere to the head (Fig. 163 on page 100).

Dry it thoroughly. Apply a new layer of soap and water (Fig. 164), so that you get a smooth surface and completely make the stocking opaque and flat.

Dry again, using the hairdryer (Fig. 165 on page 101).

Now, with a rough, red rubber sponge, pat the whole area with cured latex, applying as many layers as you need to get the surface completely flat (Fig 166).

Powder liberally, removing the excess with a soft brush. Then, with a Chinese brush, paint the area with a coat of fixative, and dry and powder it again.

Make up the face and head with a greasy, colored foundation, and then powder (Fig. 167 and 168). Apply a new layer of plastic

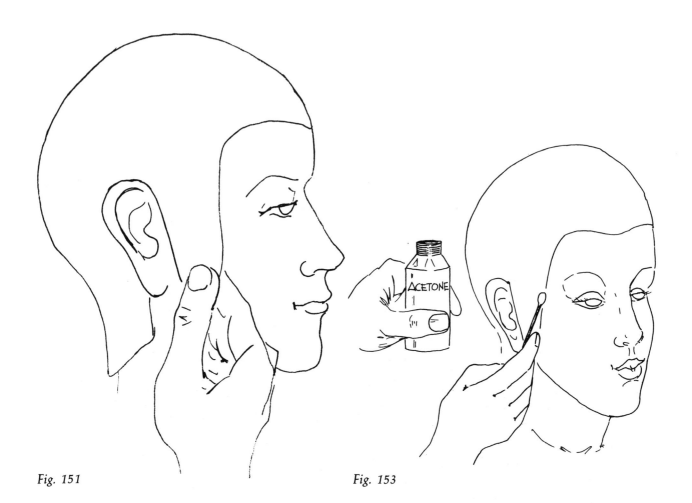

Fig. 151

Fig. 153

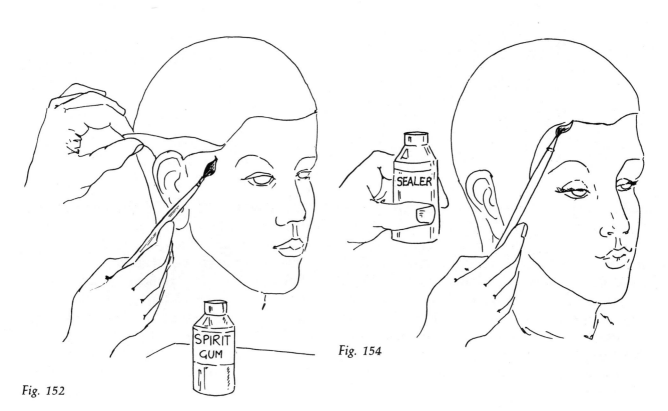

Fig. 152

Fig. 154

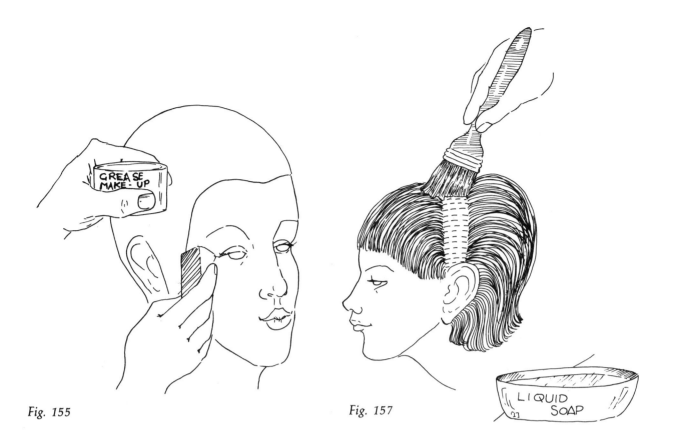

Fig. 155

Fig. 157

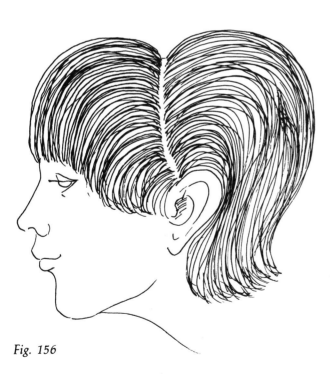

Fig. 156

fixative. Dry again with the hairdryer, spread foundation powder, and spray some fixative over it to give a "natural" shininess to the scalp (Fig. 169 on page 102).

Fig. 158

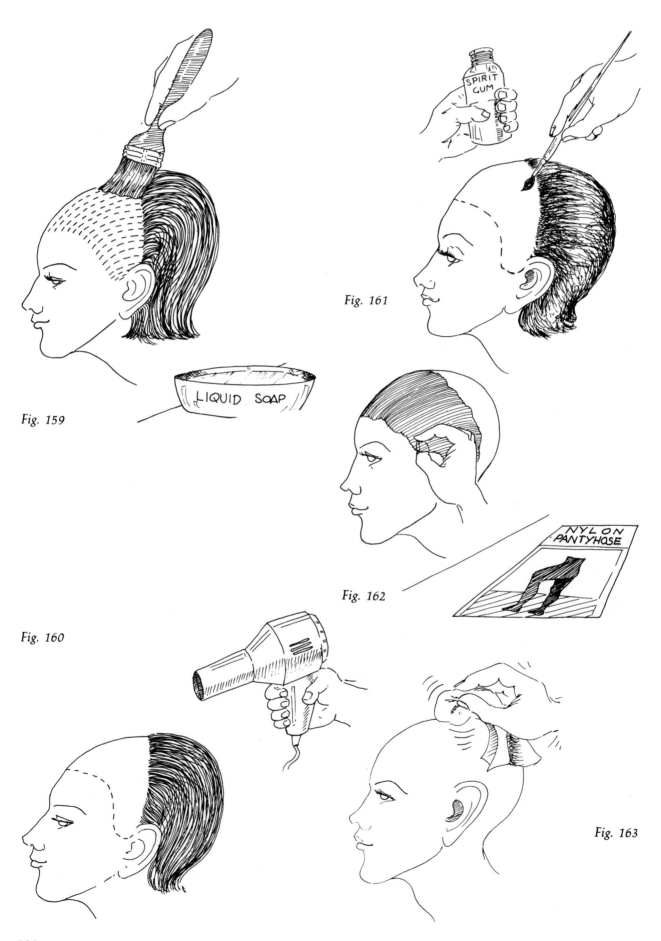

Fig. 159

LIQUID SOAP

Fig. 161

Fig. 162

NYLON PANTYHOSE

Fig. 160

SPIRIT GUM

Fig. 163

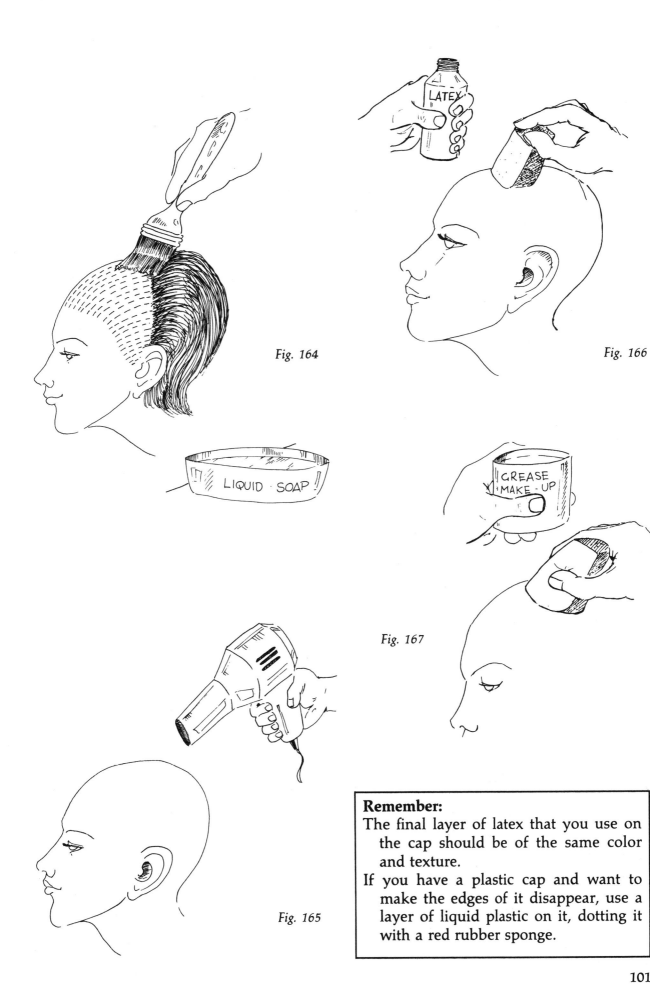

Fig. 164

Fig. 166

LIQUID · SOAP

GREASE MAKE-UP

Fig. 167

Fig. 165

Remember:
The final layer of latex that you use on the cap should be of the same color and texture.

If you have a plastic cap and want to make the edges of it disappear, use a layer of liquid plastic on it, dotting it with a red rubber sponge.

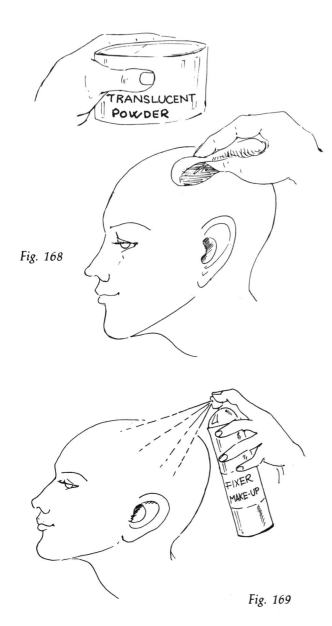

Fig. 168

Fig. 169

have to be lifted as much as possible, so it's best to do the job in three sections—and to have one person work on each part. The third person will help to dry the areas with a hairdryer by stretching the part without loosening it (Fig. 171).

When the area is dry, pat on a thin veil of translucent powder (Fig. 172) with a powder puff and then gently let it go.

For each area to be dotted, mix new adhesive paste or latex in the ceramic dish, since the adhesives dry rapidly when they come in contact with the air. Never use the same piece of sponge twice; change it after each application.

This method gives visually excellent results, but often under hot spotlights or in a warm climate the areas may come loose easily, forming ugly bubbles. Pierce these bubbles with a pin and soften the area with castor oil, which will immediately be absorbed by a layer of translucent powder.

Sometimes, instead of latex, it is better to use adhesives. In this case, before you spread the paste on the face, neck, and eventually on the hands, blend all these areas to point up flabby muscles in highlight and shadow. Then powder liberally and carefully.

Aging Skin

There is a very effective method for aging skin (which was mentioned briefly before). It consists of applying cured latex or special adhesive paste to the skin.

Start by pouring a small amount of one of these products onto a ceramic dish. Soak a rough, red rubber sponge in it and then dot it over the face. This procedure has to be followed for one area at a time, starting from the rounded edges of the face and then proceeding to the forehead, temples, nose, cheeks, jaws, and lastly, the neck (Fig. 170). All the skin and facial muscles will

Fig. 170

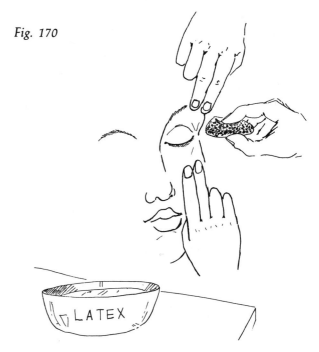

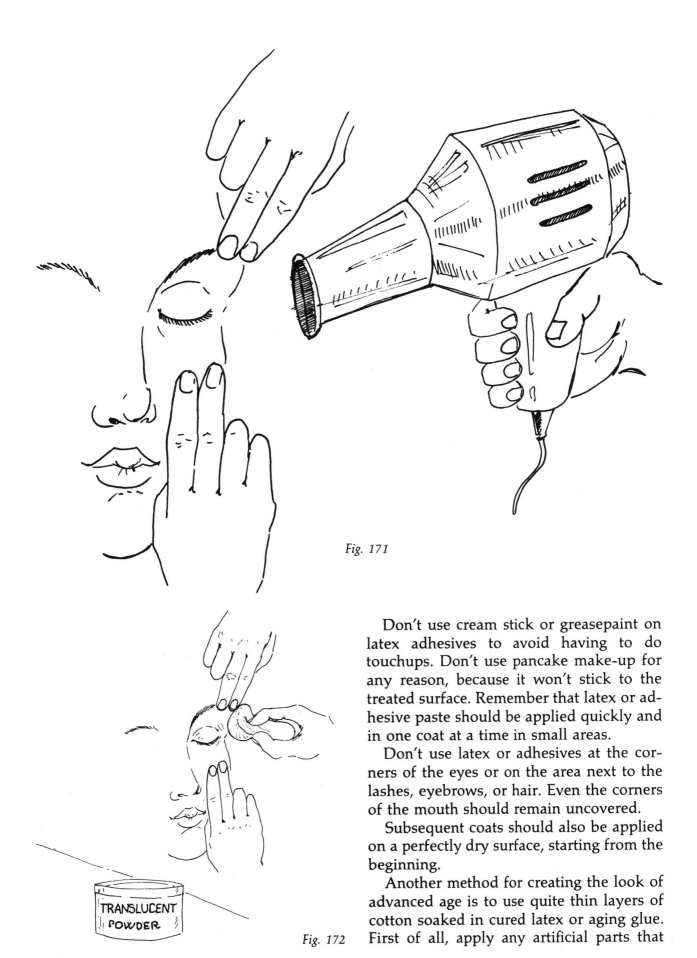

Fig. 171

Fig. 172

TRANSLUCENT POWDER

Don't use cream stick or greasepaint on latex adhesives to avoid having to do touchups. Don't use pancake make-up for any reason, because it won't stick to the treated surface. Remember that latex or adhesive paste should be applied quickly and in one coat at a time in small areas.

Don't use latex or adhesives at the corners of the eyes or on the area next to the lashes, eyebrows, or hair. Even the corners of the mouth should remain uncovered.

Subsequent coats should also be applied on a perfectly dry surface, starting from the beginning.

Another method for creating the look of advanced age is to use quite thin layers of cotton soaked in cured latex or aging glue. First of all, apply any artificial parts that

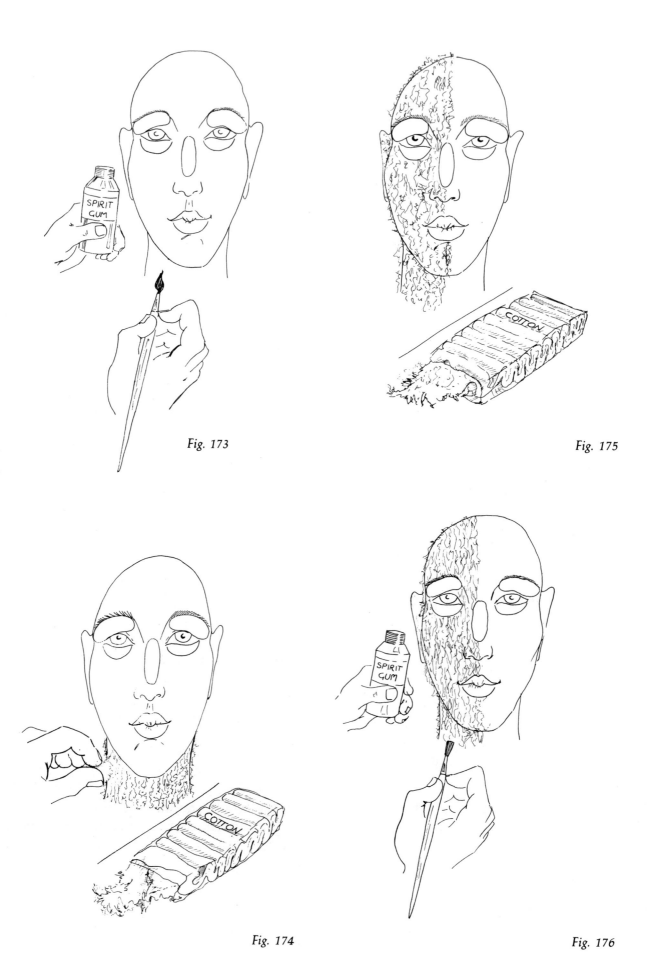

Fig. 173

Fig. 175

Fig. 174

Fig. 176

you're adding to the face. Then spread a coat of spirit gum on the area you want to cover (Fig. 173), generally starting from the neck and working your way up to the head. Cover the entire area with a thin veil of absorbent cotton (Figs. 174 and 175), which will stick to the glue. Press it down against the glue with a clean light cloth that won't unravel, or with your fingers wrapped in some pantyhose.

Repeat the same procedure on the whole face. Remove the excess as you go along with a large-toothed comb. After this, spread a heavy layer of transparent glue over the whole area that you covered with cotton. Do it with an ox-bristle brush, which you need to keep cleaning with acetone as you work (Fig. 176).

Dry it all with the hairdryer (Fig. 177), and dot it with a layer of cured latex or adhesive paste, using a red rubber sponge (Fig. 178).

When you apply latex or adhesive paste (Fig. 179), follow the same instructions as those given for the previous method.

Always apply a thin layer of plastic fixative with a red rubber sponge and dry the whole area carefully. Then apply the greasepaint or cream stick, and powder heavily to absorb excess greasiness (Figs. 180 and 181). Then you can attach beards, moustaches, false eyelashes, etc., and they will stick as long as the surface is thoroughly dry. If it's not, powder again.

Shrivelling the Skin

Many make-up artists get the shrivelled-skin effect by using thin layers of tissues with cured latex. You must gently stretch the involved area and cover it with a substantial layer of latex or adhesive paste. Rip the tissues into small pieces and place them

Fig. 177

carefully on the glued area (Fig. 182). Dry the area with a hairdryer and, after you powder it liberally, let the skin go. You'll have to shape the tissues to fit the area, tearing them slowly with your fingers—not using scissors. Then you can go ahead with the rest of your make-up as in the methods previously described (Figs. 183 and 184).

105

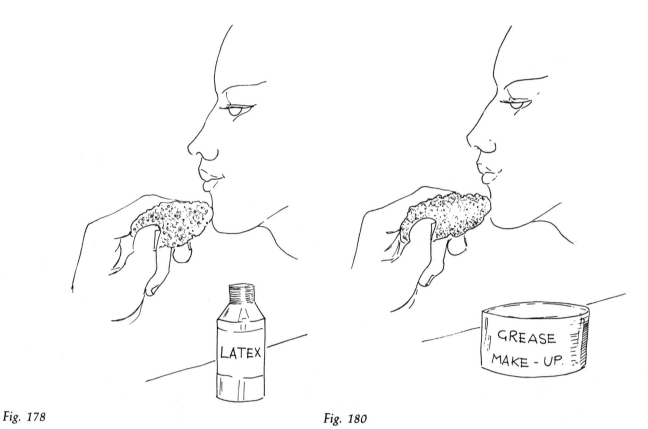

Fig. 178

Fig. 180

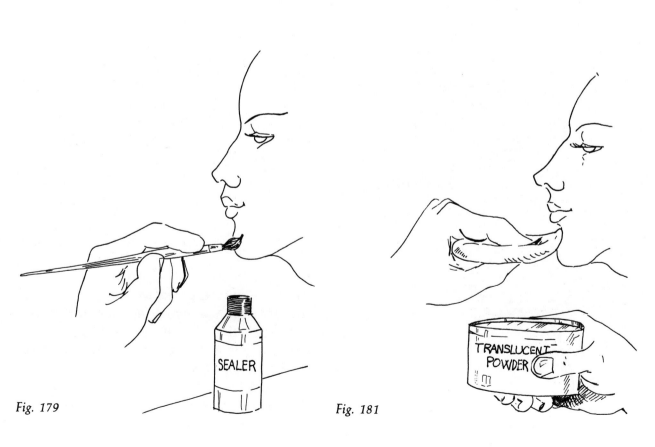

Fig. 179

Fig. 181

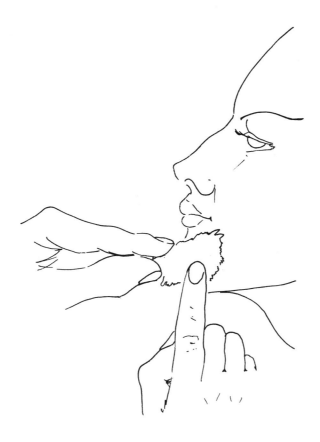

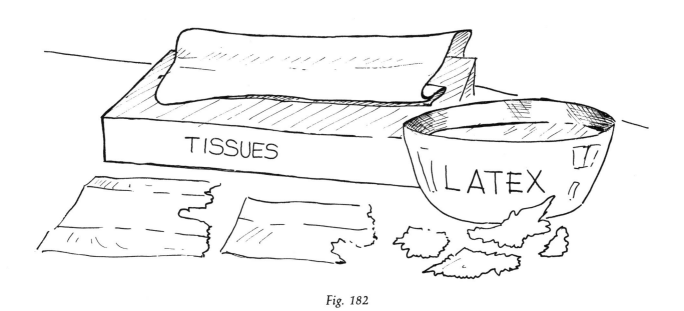

Fig. 182

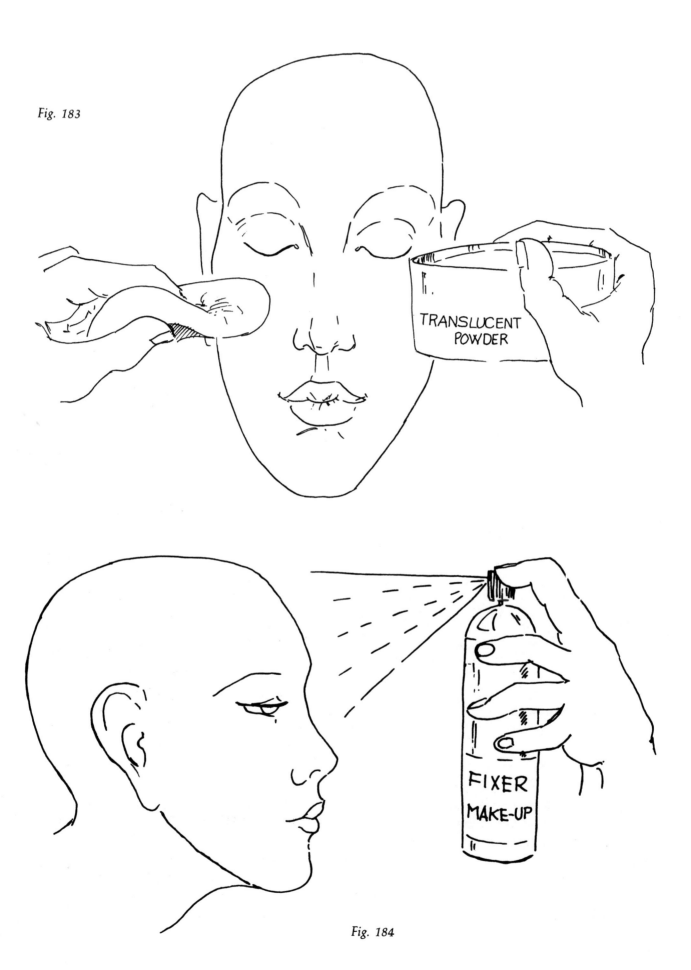

Fig. 183

TRANSLUCENT POWDER

FIXER MAKE-UP

Fig. 184

108

Special Effects

Certainly, it isn't possible to list and explain all the techniques that make-up artists use for every possible effect. However, we'll take a look at the most common ones. In the end, the effects you get will depend on your own imagination and resourcefulness. Many of the procedures that make-up artists use today were invented to fill a need—with no previous techniques on which to build.

Burns

To get the effect of a first-degree burn, dot some dark red substance with a sponge on the area. For a second-degree burn, use cured latex or adhesive paste. When dry, the plastic film will be broken and partly detached, giving the look of flaking skin.

To create a blister effect, use melted wax or smooth some industrial yellow petroleum jelly onto the skin with the back of a slightly warm spoon.

Finally, to get a third-degree burn, use both of the first two methods and then dirty the area by rubbing it with burnt cork. Add a neutral gloss to the whole area, as a final touch. And if you want, apply a little artificial blood under the loose latex film.

For really gruesome effects, mix some of the industrial yellow petroleum jelly with artificial blood and insert the paste under the loose latex film! At some points you may want to darken the skin in a brownish or bluish shade to give the look of hematomas.

Bruises

Use foamed latex casts or, if the bruises don't have to be swollen, just blend some blue or purple make-up on the area and outline it with a barely visible outline of yellow. Then apply a thin coat of almond oil or lip gloss.

Slashes

The best way is to apply a foamed latex cast. If you don't have enough time, use putty as previously described.

Even the use of collodion or adhesive paste will be successful, especially for television. Collodion is a translucent substance that hardens easily when it comes into contact with air. You apply it with a little ox-bristle brush, and you don't need to cover it with foundation.

Cuts and scars can also be obtained using the products listed above. For scars, it may be sufficient to draw the scar in with a little brush soaked in collodion or adhesive paste, so that it looks like a real scar. Then, when it is dry, draw some strokes with a reddish or dark beige pencil for defining an old scar or a fresher one.

Deep wounds can be simulated by applying cured latex onto a large area of skin and then pressing with the fingers to form two folds at the endings. Bring the two edges together and leave a slit on the central part. Spread some dark color inside, to add depth, decreasing the intensity as you move in an outward direction. On the edges add some reddish color, creating a bright base with neutral gloss. Add artificial blood with an eye dropper.

If you want to make the wound look old, remember that artificial blood will look more like the coagulated variety.

A good method for creating the illusion of obvious slashes is to soak cleansing tissues in latex or adhesive paste. Spread a layer of the adhesive on the area where you want the slash. Then add some pieces of tissue, in one strip, tearing them with your fingers, making them adhere to the skin. When the thickness in the middle is sufficient, tap the strips with a dentists' tool or paperknife in an irregular way—not neatly.

Dry with a hairdryer and apply a plastic fixative. When the slash is dry, make up the entire area with foundation. Create highlights and shadows and, if required, add some artificial blood with an eye dropper. Spray on some fixative that will brighten the whole area and make it appear more believable.

You can get the same results using cotton, instead of tissues, following the same technique.

And you can also use this method to create any prominent spots on the skin, including bags under the eyes, flabby eyelids, skin diseases, distortions, and innumerable other effects, provided that you do the work carefully and strive for perfection!

Scars

To create lasting and impressive scars, there's a very up-to-date and quick system. You do it with Knox gelatin, which is readily available in any supermarket. Proceed as follows:

Quickly dissolve a packet of Knox gelatin in a spoonful of cold water. Shape a cotton ball, leaving particularly thin edges, and soak it in the gelatin. Once it soaks up the liquid, apply it on the part where you want the scar (which should be completely clean and dry). Model it on the skin, fading out the edges perfectly. When it is all dry,

apply a layer of cured latex with a red rubber sponge.

Dry it with the hairdryer (set on warm), powder, and spread foundation on the "scar" and on the surrounding area. Powder again with some other translucent powder. As with every cast made with gelatin, remember that the heat can damage it easily—and in some cases even dissolve it!

Metallic Bodies

A very effective way to make a body look as if it's made of metal consists of applying a solution composed of the following ingredients:

20 percent pearly powder
20 percent glycerine
60 percent isopropyl alcohol

Apply the solution with a flat natural sponge. The more powder you put in, the thicker the mixture will be. This will, though, permit an easier drying once applied. It is better to avoid covering the body completely. And get all the substance off the body after about an hour and half from the time you first apply it.

To get the effect of a marble statue, the procedure remains the same, but you need to use different shades of powder or liquid foundation and apply them with a slightly damp natural sponge. You can obtain the typically bright effect of marble statues by adding a heavy coat of plastic fixative and finally spraying with brilliantine.

Lifting Flabby Muscles

For video or stage work, there's another method by which to lift flabby muscles or loose skin folds, in addition to the ones described previously.

Glue thin netting pieces in rectangular shapes, to the area you want to lift. When the area is perfectly dry, slightly lift the netting strips as much as you can without creating unattractive folds.

Never use foundation on netting. Select a

shade that is similar to the complexion of the actor, with a very thin and fine texture.

Tattoos

If you only need a tattoo for one day, you can get fine results using ball-point pens of various colors. But if you need to have exactly the same tattoo for longer, then you can use the same technique used in linoleum-block printing. Make a block by engraving the design with a little chisel on a sheet of linoleum. Then hollow out all the empty parts leaving neat and clear outlines. Using a roller covered with a layer of printers' ink, press the blotted linoleum piece hard against the area to be tattooed. Clean the edges with a cotton ball dampened in alcohol, and you'll have a perfect tattoo.

Perspiration and Tears

Spray on a mixture of water and glycerine. The exact proportions for mixing a solution to spray on the body are: 2½ parts glycerine to 1½ parts water. Almond oil can also be used, but it is very greasy. For tears, put a drop of glycerine inside the corner of the eye, or blow menthol fumes in the eye with a small glass tube.

Some make-up artists—to obtain tears for five or six minutes—squeeze orange or lemon peels in the eyes, but this gives the eye an irritating burning sensation.

To change the color of the pupil, you need to get an ophthalmologist to apply contact lenses.

Broken Capillaries

Dot the area to be made up with a dark red color and a red rubber sponge. To emphasize the effect of the broken capillaries, draw a sort of spider's net, a red-bluish web in liquid foundation on the skin. In both cases, you need to add translucent powder.

Freckles

Use the same method described above, but use a black rubber sponge, because it is more porous.

Also, small brown spots, typical of freckles, can be stressed with a pencil of the same shade and then carefully blended.

Acne

Use cured latex, dotting it on with a thin brush made of ox-bristles. Emphasize any possible redness or inflammations by blending with a reddish-brown pencil.

This technique can be used for all effects that involve blemishes, pimples, and some skin diseases.

Skin Diseases

Rashes, eczemas, and various other skin disorders are easy to simulate, oddly enough with the help of natural foods! Crumbs, grated nutmeg, sesame seeds, rye flour, and wheat flour are excellent for this purpose, and for truly gruesome effects, try oatflakes!

First apply a thin coat of liquid cured latex. Wait for a few seconds and then add the crumbs or seeds or flakes. With a large brush, spread on some more latex. Dry with a hairdryer. Powder lightly and apply the necessary base to simulate the required disease.

Scratches

Scratches are easy to simulate simply by drawing them in with a reddish-brown pencil and coating the lines with a layer of collodion, applied with a thin brush.

Note: When you use brushes with collodion you must soak them continually in pure ether.

Floppy Ears

To simulate cauliflower ears, apply little balls of plastic wax behind the ear itself or to an artificial part that you add. To flatten cauliflower ears, make them adhere to the head with a strong adhesive or with double-faced adhesive tape.

Broadening the Nose

To create a nose with large and rounded nostrils, cut off two rubber nipples from nursing bottles and carefully insert them into the nostrils.

Artificial Nails

Artificial fingernails—to be applied over natural ones with adhesive—are available everywhere and are generally translucent to allow you to color them as you wish.

But when you want to get unreal effects—such as witches' nails, for example—you may want to try this:

Draw the desired shape on a sheet of plastic. Heat the part that will fit over the real nail until it is soft enough to model on the finger. Put it on the fingers of a plastic or plaster hand and model it until you get it curved the way you want it. Stick different nails on the artificial hand with a light adhesive and carefully pass them close to the heat of a flame, keeping them an appropriate distance away so that you don't destroy them. This is necessary in order to emphasize the curve of the nails. Then remove them from the false fingers with care and glue them on the real ones.

Sometimes, for temporary effects, you can simply apply nails cut from a vegetable parchment sheet. Large nails—and various kinds of plastic nails that can reach unbelievable lengths—are also on the market.

Shaven Eyebrows

You can get the effect of shaved eyebrows in several ways. One way is to block them out with a paste fixative, after combing them upwards with a hard toothbrush. Then put on a layer of transparent glue and brush them upwards again, still with a toothbrush. Once the glue is dry, repeat the operation twice. Then pat the area, twice again, with a rough rubber sponge soaked in cured latex or adhesive paste. Then, using a Chinese brush, spread a coat of plastic fixative on the whole area, including the edges. When dry, cover with cream stick or greasepaint.

Some make-up artists, mostly for video and theatrical effects, cover the eyebrow area with a strip of organdy, shaped to fit, and liberally coated with foundation.

Another good way to do it—without wasting time—is to cover up the eyebrow area with a latex cast. To get it the right shape, apply a couple of coats of cured latex or liquid plastic on a non-porous, medium-rough surface, or on an orange peel.

Dry the film with a hairdryer (set on hot) and powder it liberally. Then remove the latex piece from the surface or orange peel. Powder it again and it will be ready to apply, using the same methods described on pages 94–99 for bald-head caps.

Oriental Eyes

The best way to make eyes look oriental is to apply a foamed latex cast. If you need to save time, there's a quick system that will work for theatre or television. Stick a thin piece of adhesive tape on a sheet of glass. Cut it as shown in Fig. 185. Avoid folding it. Now, with a honey-colored pencil, draw the shape of oriental eyes approximately the size of the actor's upper eyelid areas. Leave a sort of half moon in the lower part (Fig. 186), which will be carefully folded to leave a rounded lid outline that will look realistic.

Remove the adhesive tape from the glass and stick it on the upper part of the eye, leaving clear the brow area near the root of the nose and covering instead the outer part of the space, towards the temples (Fig. 187).

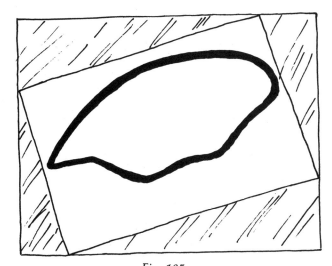

Fig. 185

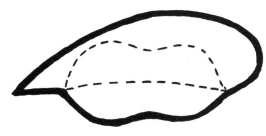

Fig. 186

Fig. 187

If necessary, pat the edges with a red rubber sponge soaked in adhesive paste. For a more realistic effect, renew the application, powder liberally, brush on a layer of plastic fixative, dry it, and powder again. Then apply greasepaint.

Correct the eyebrows, drawing or by carefully applying little tufts of hair. Make up the area with highlights and shadows, and the result will be quite satisfactory.

Heavy Eyelids

Flabby lids, which give an aged look, maybe made using the pressure-foamed-latex method.

A good way to do it quickly is to paint some coats of cured latex on a non-porous, medium-rough surface, on which you've already drawn with an eyebrow pencil the outlines of the eye and the size of the eyelid to be made up (Fig. 188). The outer edges will require only a couple of coats of latex, while the center part will need a greater thickness.

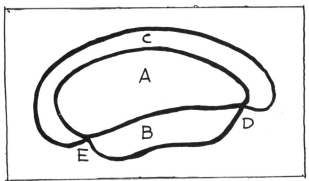

Fig. 188

In Fig. 188, area A is the part to be enlarged; area C shows the thin outlines. Area B is the part to be folded in at points D and E. You'll need to stick area B to area A to get a thicker, coarse edge that looks similar to collapsed, flabby skin.

When the latex piece is ready, powder it and apply it to the upper eyelid area using the system already explained (Fig. 189) on pages 94–99.

Fig. 189

Amazing Special Effects

How in the world did they do it?

You'll often hear that when you see movies with particularly successful special effects. This is a different kind of make-up from the classical type that is described in this book. It's the kind of make-up that

113

makes bystanders stare and reveals the Hollywood make-up artists as masters of their craft.

Think about the incredible movements of King Kong's facial expressions. Recall the realism of the make-up in *The Planet of the Apes*. Memorable special effects were achieved on the central character in Ken Russell's *Altered States*. And no movie goer could forget the extraordinary transformations in *An American Werewolf in London* and the head that literally melted in *Raiders of the Lost Ark*. The effects in these films are endlessly fascinating and vast, and a whole book could easily be written about just a few of these amazing make-up jobs.

How do the wizards of make-up do it? First of all, they use quite sophisticated techniques. They have at their command not only a great deal of knowledge about the materials they're working with, a remarkable technical ability, but they also bring years of experience in their work and an enormous amount of creativity to the solution of each different, complicated problem. This wonderful art—though it's full of unsolved riddles—is not completely without rules. In fact, there are many basic techniques for developing the elaborate, fantastic make-ups.

The first thing you need is a healthy and very patient actor. The application of an extensive job of make-up can last from four to nine hours every day the make-up needs to be applied.

Then, every make-up artist knows some fundamental elements which assist the development of his or her creative work. There are masks, first of all, that transform the actor's features completely, except for the eyes. Let's take the case of the gorilla, for example. Here the problem is twofold: The actor's face needs to be modified in relation to the gorilla's, and the basic proportions are very different. Since the actor's own features cannot be used, the first thing to be done is to apply a rigid undermask, like a skeleton. It alters the actor's features and extends the forehead and the jaws.

Then it is necessary to add a complete set of new teeth, to rebuild the palate and the tongue, and create a gorilla mouth that the actor can work using his or her own jaws.

The next step consists of covering that "skeleton" with a very elastic foamed latex mask that reproduces the gorilla's features.

At this point, in order to get truly good results, the gorilla's face needs to assume real expressions. You want the upper and lower lips to move, the forehead to knit in thought, the nose to sniff, the jaws to pulsate, the tongue to operate, and so on. For this purpose, inside the mask a series of lifts and levers run up from the nape of the neck to the particular feature. These lifts and levers are incorporated in the rigid skeleton and manipulated by the actor. This is how the gorilla becomes realistic— how he grinds his teeth, frowns, smiles, smells, sighs, saddens, and so forth.

Another basic mechanism that make-up artists use is called the air bladder. It's a soft, plastic bladder with a little tube at the end. By pumping air through the small tubes with different intensity, the bladders swell out and throb. This simple invention can be used in many cases to create extremely exciting effects.

For instance, look at the changes which the protagonist in *Altered States* undergoes. Here the use of air bladders is fundamental. During one scene in the film, the protagonist looks with horror at the tremendous transformation of his arm and abdomen, which blow out and throb. The bladder parts are fixed on the points where the transformations are required, while the small tubes (well concealed from view) are attached to air pumps.

Furthermore, the body area in which the air bladders are located are reconstructed with a thin latex covering. A cast is fixed over the air bladders to hide them. At this point, arm and abdomen appear normal and no one would ever suspect the presence of machinery! When air is pumped into the small tubes, the bladders blow out and make the artificial skin swell, creating the illusion of a horrible pulsation of the made-up area. These two techniques—the artificial part (cast) and the air bladder—are basic to a very complex make-up.

Add to this the fact that each make-up artist, faced with many mind-boggling problems, must invent something different which brings together not only the standard materials such as foamed latex, glass fibre, and resin, but also a series of mechanisms that we never even hear about in a standard make-up course. For this reason, the most valued wizards of special effects hire a staff of specialized technicians in many areas, who can help them reach the most spectacular results.

Take the case of the werewolf transformation in *An American Werewolf in London.* In that film, technical expertise reached a high point. Thanks to a quite easy and ingenious combination of masks, air bladders, traditional make-up, and machines, we see the chief character slowly changing into a ghastly monster. Hands and feet grow longer, becoming paws; the body grows more and more deformed, the face lengthens and reveals terrible fangs, and the dismayed audience cannot possibly perceive what's truly happening.

For the above-mentioned film, make-up magician Rick Baker, building on the experience of such masters as Dick Smith, Stuart Freeborn, and John Chambers, brilliantly succeeded, and he was awarded—for the first time in the history of films—an Oscar for special make-up.

What more is there to say than this? It's about time an official award was made to make-up artists, especially when their work is a major factor in the success of the film.

Hair and Beards

Before discussing problems relating to hair for film, video, and photography, it is important to know how to measure head and beard in order to supply the wigmaker with accurate information.

Measurements of the Head (Fig. 190)
A. Around the head
B. From the front hairline to the nape of the neck, over the top of the head
C. From sideburn to sideburn, over the crown of the head
D. From ear to ear, over the top of the head
E. From ear to ear, across the forehead at the hairline
F. From the bottom of one ear to the bottom of the other, around the back of the neck
G. From temple to temple, around the back of the head
H. From the bottom of one sideburn to the bottom of the other, on the top of the head

Measurements of the Beard (Fig. 190)
1. From sideburn to sideburn, across the point of the chin
2. From one side of the mouth to the end of the jawbone, under the ear
3. From the bottom of the lower lip to the ending point of the beard
4. Across the front of chin, below the lower lip, end to end

Types of Hair

Many different types of hair are available to the make-up artist: crepe hair, crepe wool, horse hair, Angora goat hair, and human hair. Most make-up artists use crepe hair and crepe wool for films and video, but skeins of real and artificial hair are also used for constructing wigs. Most of the types of hair mentioned above are sold braided and can be mixed together to create beards, moustaches, and special hair effects.

Full-length Beards

It may seem, to all appearances, a simple matter, but the application of hair to create a realistic-looking full-length beard requires remarkable skill and accuracy. Crepe wool is used more in television and theatre than in films, where crepe hair is more popular. Good results can be achieved with

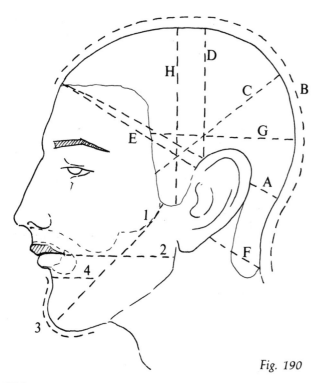

Fig. 190

both kinds, and they are used as follows:

1. Untie the braid a bit at a time, cutting only the length of hair you need.

2. With moistened fingers, smooth out the stiff, curled hairs, taking care not to wet them too much and leaving a bit of a wave in them—just enough for them to look real (Figs. 191 and 192).

3. Iron the hair (Fig. 193). Many make-up artists use steam irons or electric

Fig. 193

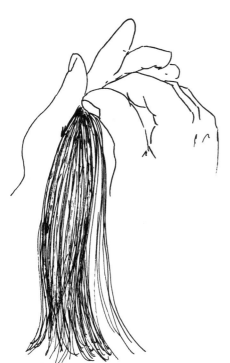

Fig. 191

Fig. 192

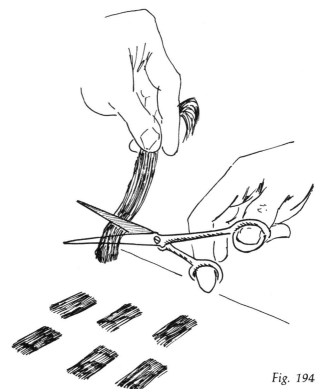

Fig. 194

machines provided with special ironing rolls. As you iron, keep cutting the hair into the lengths required for the beard until you have enough of them (Fig. 194).

4. Be sure to control the length so that you don't have to work with hairs of different sizes (Fig. 195).

5. Apply an adhesive—such as spirit gum—to the areas of the face and neck where you want the beard (Fig. 196). Apply it only on the area that will be covered immediately afterward, and not on large facial areas (Fig. 197).

6. Begin applying hairs to the face in

117

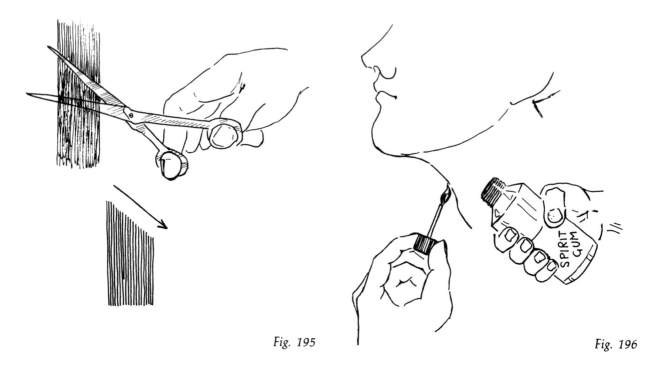

Fig. 195

Fig. 196

small tufts and in limited areas (Fig. 198). When you're creating a full-length beard, always apply the first tufts on the chin, continuing to the neckbone—and from the jawline towards the cheeks (Fig. 199).

Apply moustaches from the outer towards the inner part of the face—and sideburns from the lower part in an upward direction (Fig. 200).

This part of the operation has to be done with a tremendous amount of patience and care. As you work, pat and trim off the excess adhesive and hair with an old nylon stocking that is not unravelled (Fig. 201). As you proceed, use hairdresser's scissors to help attach and trim the locks (Fig. 202). Keep a bowl with some acetone nearby to clean the points of

Fig. 197

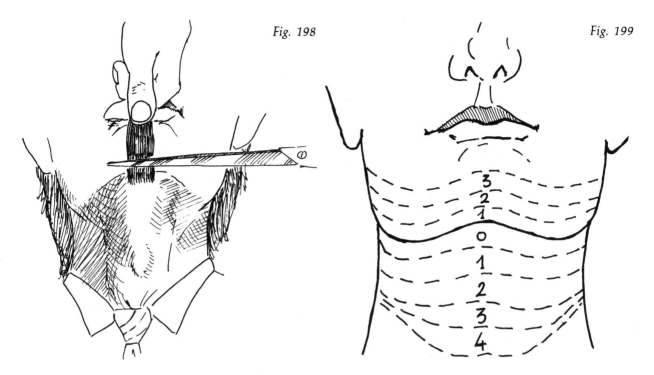

Fig. 198   *Fig. 199*

the scissors, because the adhesive will stick to them. Remember, from time to time, to pat the false beard with the nylon stocking (or any clean cloth in good condition), so that it adheres more firmly to the face.

To create a more realistic effect, mix different colors of hair, always remaining in the same range of shades. And keep in mind that the area where the beard line begins is always lighter than successive areas.

When you apply beards, moustaches, and sideburns that are constructed on net, using a system we'll examine a bit later on when we talk about attaching wigs, be sure to cover the edges of the net with small amounts of crepe hair (Fig. 203) for best results.

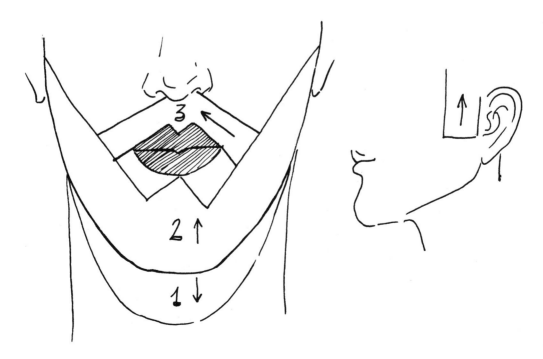

Fig. 200

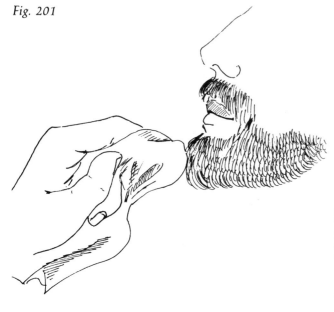

Fig. 201

7. When the work is finished, apply hairspray sparingly where needed, so that the beard will take shape and look bright. Human hair always has a light and natural shine to it, so select a bright hairspray. *Never* spray crepe hair and wool with water or oily solutions, because if you do, the hairs will stick together, become too smooth, and look phony.

If you want to comb a crepe beard, use a large-tooth comb (Fig. 204) and take great care! It's easy to run into annoying problems.

Fig. 204

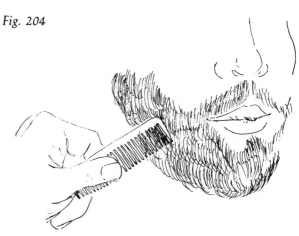

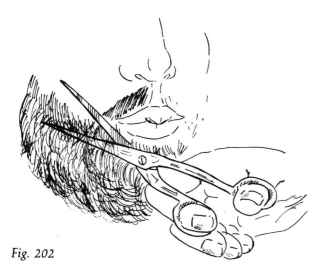

Fig. 202

If you want to shape and curl the beard, use small curling irons on it before applying the hairspray. If you do use them, be sure to control the heat so that it is neither too hot nor too cool. For best results, this requires patience, care, and experience.

There are other ways to prepare beards and moustaches. You may want to build up a full-length beard on a latex base which has been constructed on the face of the person who will wear it. Test out the latex color first, if you decide to do this, to make sure the color is similar to the complexion of the actor in question. It's very easy to choose too dark a color and then, when the latex dries, have too dark a latex mask.

Create a latex mask as follows:

1. Apply a coat of latex on the entire beard area, stopping about one-fifth of an inch before the edges of the hair growth.

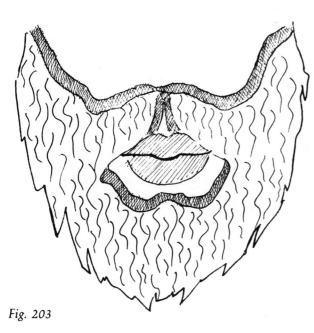

Fig. 203

2. Attach small pieces of net on this surface, until they stick firmly.
3. Dry the area with a hairdryer.
4. Liberally apply another coat of latex.
5. Dry again with hot air.
6. Pat with plenty of powder.
7. Continue using the same techniques previously described for creating the full-length beard.

Once the work is over and the false beard has been shaped the way you want it, carefully add some tufts of hair on the outer edges to make the beard line more natural.

To remove the beard after the performance, delicately separate it from the face, and powder it inside and on the latex edges, to prevent it from curling up.

To reuse the beard, attach it to the face with spirit gum.

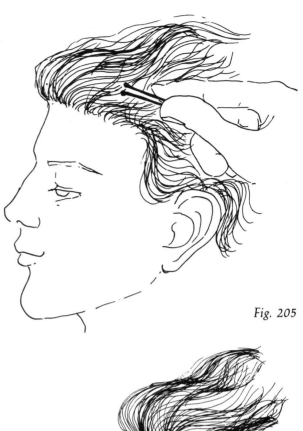

Fig. 205

Wigs

To correctly put on a wig, first you must flatten the real hair of the actor in question. Divide long hair into sections, gather it in flat coils, and pin it down against the head with crossed hairpins. For short hair, gather it in tufts and pin it down with hairpins kept together with little rubber bands.

In either case, the next step is to fit a nylon stocking over the hair (use the strongest part of it). Pull the stocking down until it almost covers the hairline, then fasten it down with long hairpins.

The end of the stocking must be stretched and knotted or fastened with hairpins. At this point, you're ready to put on the wig. Place it right on the center of the head, delicately pulling it backwards and forwards until the edge of the netting reaches the area immediately past the actual hairline.

Fasten the wig on with hairpins. Then, carefully lifting the edge of the netting, dot the skin with a brush moistened in adhesive (Figs. 205 and 206).

To make the netting adhere perfectly along the hairline, press it down with a

Fig. 206

clean cloth. Before you do it, make sure no hair is apt to come out from underneath. If it is starting to, tuck it backwards using the tail of a comb.

To eliminate any excess shininess of the glue or any yellowish color it may leave on the skin, pat the area with a nylon stocking immediately after you apply the adhesive.

Some of my colleagues prefer to make up the face after the wig has been put on. Others (myself included) think it's better to put the wig on after the make-up is complete. False hairpieces—such as moustaches, beards, sideburns, and eyebrows—have to be applied afterwards as well. Be sure that your tools and materials are scrupulously clean. Take painstaking care in removing make-up residue from wigs and hairpieces every time you use them. You can do this by placing the netting over a clean cloth and going over it with a brush that has been moistened in acetone.

Make sure the edge of the netting is not larger than three-eighths of an inch. If it is, cut the excess netting off with sharp scissors.

When you finish the make-up, before you apply moustache or beard, it is essential to use a translucent powder to dry the areas where you want to stick the hair. Of course, you can eliminate any excess powder by going over the face lightly with a special brush with soft, thick bristles.

Unshaven Beards

To create the look of an unshaven beard, cut up crepe hair into very small lengths so that you end up with a sort of hair "dust" (Fig. 207). Then apply a coat of adhesive paste to the whole area where the beard should be and pat on the cut-up crepe hair with a large brush (Figs. 208 and 209). Remove excess hair by delicately patting the area with a clean cloth. Touch up the beard by pressing the face lightly with a moistened sponge.

Fig. 207

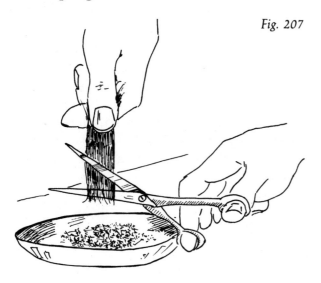

Hair Tips

Whatever the problem is with hair—whether you have to iron it, arrange an elaborate hairdo, or dye it—it pays to work with a good hairdresser who handles all these jobs easily and well. If you try to dye hair yourself, using colored hairsprays, you'll get an unattractive, artificial look that may present unexpected difficulties. Only use that kind of artificial coloring for temporary effects in the theatre and for television and photography. When you use the hairsprays, hold them seven to eight inches away from the hair.

A good way to get the effect of dark, frizzy hair is to spray on a dry shampoo before you apply silver hairspray.

If you're working in films, it is best to consult a skilled hairdresser. Never go on location without having someone dress the wigs you'll be taking with you. Let the hairstylist solve all the hair problems ahead of time, so that all you need to do is give last-minute help. It's best to use wigs only if necessary, because if they're not perfectly applied, they can look unnatural, and the hairline of a wig, especially in films, can become painfully obvious. This is one of the best reasons for working with a good hairstylist who knows how to do period hairdos without having to resort to wigs.

Draw some sketches—or snap some photos—at the beginning of each project, in order to have comparisons which can prove very useful for a better knowledge of your work.

Cleaning

It can't be overemphasized that you must keep supplies and equipment very clean. Even your make-up kit must be cleaned often to keep material in it in good condition. Wash brushes with water and mild shampoo, taking care not to let water inside the handle that grips the bristles. Rinse the bristles thoroughly to get all the shampoo out. Clean sponges with warm water to

Fig. 208

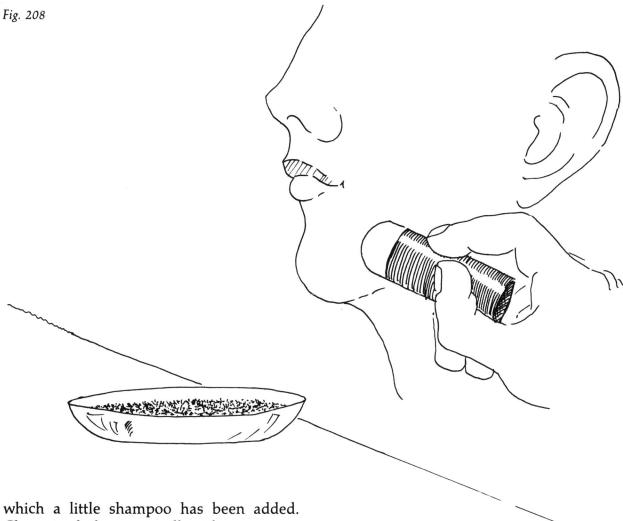

which a little shampoo has been added. Chamois cloths are excellent for removing make-up from the face, but you need to wash them.

To remove adhesive from false eyelashes, use your fingers and a small brush dipped in acetone. Acetone is algo good for cleaning any latex casts, but use it with care.

For removing heavy make-up from the face, use a good cleansing oil, almond oil, or special cleansing cream.

You can remove hairspray with a few brush strokes while you'll need to shampoo to remove spray colors. Latex applications on the skin will come off easily with the help of hot compresses.

Remove grease or wax residue with soap and water and finally with a cotton ball dipped in isopropyl alcohol.

Teeth blocked out with colored enamel will become white again if you rub them with a cotton ball dipped in alcohol. Liquid rubber residue can be removed with acetone. Artificial blood will disappear with soap and water—even from clothes—while plastic blood used for old wounds requires acetone.

To remove tattoos, wipe the skin with a cotton ball dipped in isopropyl alcohol.

Other products, specially prepared for removing problem substances, are available from make-up suppliers and other special sources.

Adhesives

A wide range of adhesives are available. Many of them are excellent for make-up purposes, others are less good, and some are absolutely unsuitable. The major types

Fig. 209

are liquid glue, transparent adhesive called spirit gum (with long-lasting adhesive, but it needs to be used with care because of its shininess), and white, milky-type latex adhesive. This latter type is used in areas where it's important that it doesn't show when it dries. It is excellent for attaching false eyelashes and for artifically aging the skin. The application of this sort of adhesive paste sometimes causes technical complications: very often, in fact, the paste doesn't hold.

Film and television make-up artists use plenty of the above-mentioned products for different purposes, and choosing between them in a subjective matter. In any case, every professional make-up artist experiments with all sorts of adhesives and learns by trial and error the qualities and limitations of each product.

Advice and Recipes

Classifying make-up colors is risky—if not impossible—because they vary among different manufacturers. And add to that the changes that take place when lights and filters are used, and you can imagine the extent of the problem. The only way is to learn through experience, which you'll soon acquire. Remember, you can learn many useful things by experimenting on your own.

If you live in a place where it's impossible to get the right colors for a special make-up, there's a simple but satisfactory trick: Thinly grate pigments from pastels onto a sheet of sandpaper. Then mix them with a bit of castor oil, until you get a thick, richly colored paste that you can apply.

When you have to make up dry or over-tanned skin, apply a thin coat of castor oil on the face. It will be helpful in getting the base to adhere to the skin, and therefore last longer, with a more natural look.

To eliminate the bluish halo under the eyes or the shadow of a beard or obvious tattoo marks, mix some pink-orange colors with the foundation and spread it liberally on the area involved. The results are surprising.

To lighten brown, olive, or other darkish skin, you may want to use a heavy foundation in a yellow shade, called an "underbase." This technique is valuable when you want to use a light-colored base but want to avoid colors that change the overall skin tone.

For whitening dark hair, color it a light yellow or blond before you spray it with a white color. Or you can use a beige-, yellow-, or orange-colored hair spray, as mentioned on page 32.

To apply pancake make-up most successfully, remember to moisten the sponge (not too much) in a solution composed of three parts water to one part astringent lotion.

To make false pieces adhere to the skin, during application, keep patting the latex edges down with a small moistened natural sponge. That way you'll keep them from wrinkling and rolling.

To get the make-up to stick better to false pieces, it's a good idea to spread a light coat of some kind of gel or petroleum jelly on the area, powder, then apply foundation.

Before applying any kind of adhesive on the skin, always use a light base coat of a non-oily emulsion or liquid foundation. This will act as a setting agent for the latex film.

To get putty to keep its shape on a particular area, apply a thin layer of latex on top of it, and on the areas bordering it. To obtain a putty color similar to skin color, add a small amount of cream foundation to the plastic wax after you knead it with your fingers to make it supple.

Latex or other adhesive substances that may fall off during a take because of the heat of the lights can be reattached quickly with a bit of spirit gum. Then, afterward, another application of latex or adhesive paste will secure it.

To simulate a bruise with make-up, remember the following rule: If it's an old bruise, it should be yellowish, and if it's new, it should be reddish.

For covering flat scars, which are slippery and on which make-up won't adhere easily—before spreading the base—apply a light coat of spirit gum. Let it dry, pat on a thin coat of powder, and proceed with the usual make-up.

If you can't find any good artificial blood, you can make it yourself by mixing a bit of red vermilion pigment with some petroleum jelly and castor oil in an enamel bowl. Warm it over a medium flame, stirring until the color melts with the oil. When it cools it is ready to use.

To create a product that will age skin artificially, mix the following ingredients:
1 teaspoon talcum powder
1 teaspoon powdered cake make-up
1 tablespoon petroleum jelly
1 tablespoon hot water

Stir until all the elements are thoroughly integrated and apply it as described on page 102.

Some film and television make-up artists, when aging skin, use abundant coats of castor oil. First they apply adhesive paste, and then, keeping the skin stretched, they paint on castor oil with a large brush, in order to let the latex film set and soften. At this point they slowly loosen the stretched part and proceed with the make-up job. At the end of this procedure, they powder abundantly. This is a good technique for making latex adhere longer, but it leaves excess greasiness, which will make the make-up smudge when subjected to hot lights. Experiment with this system yourself for best results.

Index